Sexuality and Mind

PSYCHOANALYTIC CROSSCURRENTS
General Editor: Leo Goldberger

SEXUALITY AND MIND

The Role of the Father and the Mother in the Psyche

JANINE CHASSEGUET-SMIRGEL

New York University Press
New York and London

We wish to acknowledge gratefully the following who have generously given permission to reprint from copyrighted works:

"Freud and Female Sexuality: The consideration of some blind spots in the exploration of the 'Dark Continent.'"
Presented as part of a Dialogue on "Freud and Female Sexuality" at the 29th International Psycho-Analytical Congress, London, July 1975.
Published with the kind permission of the *International Journal of Psycho-Analysis* where it appeared in 1976, vol. 57, pp. 275–286.
"The Feminity of the Analyst in Professional Practice."
Presented at the 33rd International Congress, Madrid, July 1983.
Published with the kind permission of the *International Journal of Psycho-Analysis* where it appeared in 1984, vol. 65, pp. 169–178.
"The Submissive Daughter," translated by Maisey Paget.
Presented at the Congress of the Canadian Society, Montreal, May 1984.
"A 'Special Case' (On Transference Love in the Male)," translated by Philip Slotkine.
Presented in a shorter version at the European English-Speaking Congress, London, October 1984 and in a complete version at a Symposium on "The Father" organized by the Professor Stork in Munich, 1984.
"The Archaic Matrix of the Oedipus Complex," translated by Maisey Paget.
André Ballard Lecture, Columbia University, New York, December 1984.
"The Archaic Matrix of the Oedipus Complex in Utopia," translated by Maisey Paget.
André Ballard Seminar, New York, December 1984.
"The Green Theater: Essay on Collective Manifestations of Unconscious Guilt."
Presented at a Symposium on Depression, Institute of the Paris Psycho-Analytic Society, Paris, September 1985.
"The Paradox of the Freudian Method."
Presented at the celebration of the 25th Anniversary of the "Sigmund Freud Institut," Frankfurt, December 1985.

Library of Congress Cataloging-in-Publication Data

Chasseguet-Smirgel, Janine, 1928–
    Sexuality and mind.

    (Psychoanalytic crosscurrents)
    Bibliography: p.
    Includes index.
    1. Sex (Psychology) 2. Father and child. 3. Mother and child. 4. Psychoanalysis. 5. Freud, Sigmund, 1856–1939. I. Title. II. Series.
BF692.C52 1986   155.3   86-12635
ISBN 0-8147-1400-5

In the garden of the world, oriental myths recognize two trees, to which they give a universal significance, which is both fundamental and opposed. The first is the olive tree. The oil from its fruits is used to anoint the foreheads of kings, so they may have long life. It is the tree of life, sacred to the sun. The solar principle, virile, intellectual, lucid, is linked to its essence. . . . The other is the fig tree. Its fruits are full of sweet, red seeds, and whosoever eats of them dies. . . .

The world of the day, of the sun, is the world of the mind . . . It is a world of knowledge, liberty, will, of principles and moral purpose, of the fierce opposition of reason to human fatality . . . At least half of the human heart does not belong to this world, but to the other, to that of the night and lunar gods. It is an infinitely more tempting world for poets to write about . . . not a world of the mind but of the soul, not a virile, generative world, but a cherishing, maternal one, not a world of being and lucidity, but one in which the warmth of the womb nurtures the Unconscious.

—Thomas Mann "Die Baüme im Garten" (1930) ["The Trees of Eden"]

Contents

Foreword

The *Psychoanalytic Crosscurrents* series presents selected books and monographs that reveal the growing intellectual ferment within and across the boundaries of psychoanalysis.

Freud's theories and grand-scale speculative leaps have been found wanting, if not disturbing, from the very beginning and have led to a succession of derisive attacks, shifts in emphasis, revisions, modifications, and extensions. Despite the chronic and, at times, fierce debate that has characterized psychoanalysis, not only as a movement but also as a science, Freud's genius and transformational impact on the twentieth century have never been seriously questioned. Recently psychoanalytic thought has been subjected to dramatic reassessments under the sway of contemporary currents in the history of ideas, philosophy of science, epistemology, structuralism, critical theory, semantics, and semiology as well as in sociobiology, ethology, and neurocognitive science. Not only is Freud's place in intellectual history being meticulously scrutinized, his texts, too, are being carefully read, explicated, and debated within a variety of conceptual frameworks and sociopolitical contexts.

The legacy of Freud is perhaps most notably evident within the narrow confines of psychoanalysis itself, the "impossible profession" that has served as the central platform for the promulgation of official orthodoxy. But Freud's contributions—his original radical thrust— reach far beyond the parochial concerns of the clinical psychoanalyst as clinician. His writings touch a wealth of issues, crossing traditional boundaries—be they situated in the biological, social, or humanistic spheres—that have profoundly altered our conception of the individual and society.

A rich and flowering literature, falling under the rubric of "applied psychoanalysis," came into being, reached its zenith many decades ago, and then almost vanished. Early contributors to this literature, in addition to Freud himself, came from a wide range of backgrounds both within and outside the medical/psychiatric field; many later became psychoanalysts themselves. These early efforts were characteristically reductionistic in their attempt to extrapolate from psychoanalytic theory (often the purely clinical theory) to explanations of phenomena lying at some distance from the clinical. Over the years, academic psychologists, educators, anthropologists, sociologists, political scientists, philosophers, jurists, literary critics, art historians, artists, and writers, among others (with or without formal psychoanalytic training) have joined in the proliferation of this literature.

The intent of the *Psychoanalytic Crosscurrents* series is to apply psychoanalytic ideas to topics that may lie beyond the narrowly clinical, but its essential conception and scope are quite different. The present series eschews the reductionistic tendency to be found in much traditional "applied psychoanalysis." It acknowledges not only the complexity of psychological phenomena but also the way in which they are embedded in social and scientific contexts that are constantly changing. It calls for a dialectical relationship to earlier theoretical views and conceptions rather than a mechanical repetition of Freud's dated thoughts. The series affirms that contributions to and about psychoanalysis have come from many directions. It is designed as a forum for the multidisciplinary studies that intersect with psychoanalytic thought but without the requirement that psychoanalysis necessarily be the starting point or, indeed, the center focus. The criteria for inclusion in the series are that the work be significantly informed by psychoanalytic thought or that it be aimed at furthering our understanding of psychoanalysis in its broadest meaning as theory, practice, and sociocultural phenomenon; that it be of current topical interest and that it provide the critical reader with contemporary insights; and above all, that it be high-quality scholarship, free of obsolete dogma, banalization, and empty jargon. The author's professional identity and particular theoretical orientation matter only to the extent that such facts may serve to frame the work for the reader, alerting him or her to inevitable biases of the author.

The Psychoanalytic Crosscurrents Series presents an array of works from the multidisciplinary domain in an attempt to capture the ferment of scholarly activities at the core as well as at the boundaries of psychoanalysis. The books and monographs are from a variety of sources:

authors will be psychoanalysts–traditional, neo- and post-Freudian, existential, object-relational, Kohutian, Lacanian, etc.—social scientists with quantitative or qualitative orientations to psychoanalytic data, and scholars from the vast diversity of approaches and interests that make up the humanities. The series entertains works on critical comparisons of psychoanalytic theories and concepts as well as philosophical examinations of fundamental assumptions and epistemic claims that furnish the base for psychoanalytic hypotheses. It includes studies of psychoanalysis as literature (discourse and narrative theory) as well as the application of psychoanalytic concepts to literary criticism. It will serve as an outlet for psychoanalytic studies of creativity and the arts. Works in the cognitive science and neuroscience will be included to the extent that they address some fundamental psychoanalytic tenet, such as the role of dreaming and other forms of unconscious mental processes.

It should be obvious that an exhaustive enumeration of the types of works that might fit into the *Psychoanalytic Crosscurrents* series is pointless. The studies comprise a lively and growing literature as a unique domain; books of this sort are frequently difficult to classify or catalog. Suffice it to say that the overriding aim of the editor of this series is to serve as a conduit for the identification of the outstanding yield of that emergent literature and to foster its further unhampered growth.

Leo Goldberger
Professor of Psychology
New York University

Acknowledgments

I have written a book on the Ego Ideal, which represents a destiny of narcissism. This follows the studies Béla Grunberger has devoted to the concept of narcissism, the first of which was written in 1956. I have few illusions concerning man's ability to provide himself with his own narcissistic nourishment. He needs others to hold out a mirror so that he may contemplate what he sees there without feelings of self-hatred or self-adoration; deprived of this, he would die, or cease to progress. First of all, therefore, I wish to thank those who have encouraged me to continue, showing interest in my work, engaging in lively discussion and offering timely criticism: Béla Grunberger, the colleagues who invited me as André Ballard Lecturer in December 1984, and those with whom I discussed my essay "The Green Theater" in New York in November 1985.

I also wish to thank Professor Leo Goldberger for his confidence.

The exchanges that have taken place with Kitty Moore, Senior Editor, and Despina Papazoglou, Managing Editor, have made it a pleasure to work with them.

Lastly, I wish to express my gratitude to my translators, especially my friends Maisey Paget in London and Janet Cheng in Paris.

Janine Chasseguet-Smirgel
Paris, December 1985

Introduction

When I was asked by Dr. Leo Goldberger to write a book for his series *Psychoanalytic Crosscurrents,* a request I was very honored to receive, I immediately thought of a series of articles I had recently written and which, for the most part, were unpublished. Yet it was not until I began to reread them that I became increasingly aware of a more or less unconscious strand that ran through them, an awareness which became more and more apparent as I progressed in my reading.

The articles included in this volume have, all but one, been written since 1983. In order to allow the reader to follow the course of my thoughts, I felt I should begin with a much older article entitled "Freud and Female Sexuality: The Consideration of Some Blind Spots in the Exploration of the 'Dark Continent,'" written in 1975. About twenty years ago I edited a book called *Female Sexuality,* published in France (Paris: Payot, 1964) and translated in 1970 in America (Ann Arbor: Michigan University Press). A new edition was published in London (Virago) some years ago and Karnac Books has just republished it. This volume has also been published in several other languages. It was, in fact, one of the first, or perhaps even *the* first, post-war attempt at bringing psychoanalytic theory on female sexuality into focus, as well as Freud's views on the question. As a contributor to and editor of this book, I was invited to present a paper in 1975 at the Congress of the International Psycho-Analytical Association held in London. This paper constituted part of a dialogue on the subject with my American colleague, Dr. Burness Moore.

Between the publication of *Female Sexuality* in France and the Congress in London, many things happened, in particular the French student rebellion of May 1968, followed by the heyday of the feminist movement and an efflorescence of multiple ideologies. In France, to limit myself to my cultural context and to refrain, momentarily at least, from trespassing beyond the field of psychoanalysis, I recall the anti-Oedipal ideology propounded by G. Deleuze and F. Guattari in *L'anti-Oedipe* (Paris: Editions de Minuit, 1972), a new avatar of Wilhelm Reich. Appearing in precisely the year I presented my paper at the London Congress, it prompted me to write a book with Béla Grunberger in which we dealt with the "perennial return" of Wilhelm Reich (*Freud or Reich?* Yale University Press). In fact, one of the latent themes of that book, as in the work of Reich, is the disappearance of the father and of his function as the *separation* between mother and child. In one of the last books he wrote, *Ether, God and the Devil* (1949), Wilhelm Reich postulates the union between man and God, identified with the Cosmos. The "Ego" has simply disappeared. We find this also in Deleuze and Guattari, who postulate the "co-extension of man and Nature." Their model of an unmutilated human being is the schizophrenic: "The Ego can be compared to mummy-daddy; the schizoprenic has long since ceased to believe in it" (French edition, p. 30). Chapter 6 of our book ends with the following statement about Reich: "Yet, behind the desire for a grand coupling with God the Father, we find, as you may have guessed, the fantasy of dissolution into the Cosmos, a fusion with the primary object, the Mother."

During this period many French and European intellectuals (Sartre, Moravia, Macciocchi, for instance) gave themselves over to whole-hearted support of Maoism, despite the negative reports provided by Simon Leys (*Les habits neufs du Président Mao* [*Chairman Mao's New Clothes*] in 1971 and *Ombres Chinoises* [*Chinese Shadows*] in 1974). Their disappointment was indeed real when, after five years filled with sinister, perverse and sanguinary exploits, the "Cultural Revolution" finally came to an end. Maoism and the Cultural Revolution, are founded, among other things, on a sanctification of the peasantry, a class whose "purity" is undoubtedly related to its contact with the earth, Mother Nature. In April, 1975, Cambodia became the scene for one of the worst terrors the world has known since Auschwitz; a terror unleashed in the name of an ideology close to that from which the Chinese Cultural Revolution drew its inspiration. It strove for a return to Nature and demonstrated active hatred of the city dweller.

At that time, I did not associate this new cult of Nature, the disappearance of the father's image, of the ego, on the one hand, with my own essay on "Freud and Female Sexuality," on the other. It is only now that these connections stare me in the face. At the time our newspapers said little about the Khmers Rouges and their horrifying exploits. China was still very much admired by both the Right (one of the books to sing the praises of China was written by a minister in the de Gaulle regime) and the Left.

But the times have changed, for on September 2, 1985 Patrick Sabatier quite calmly wrote an article highly critical of the Cultural Revolution and published it in *Libération,* a leftist newspaper founded in 1973 by Jean-Paul Sartre to serve the Maoist cause. This newspaper has since changed its position, but the article quoted below contains no mea culpa for its past opinions.

> Deng Junior [Deng Xiaoping's son] is reluctant to speak about the Cultural Revolution, the movement launched by President Mao which devastated China between 1966 and 1971, killing thousands upon thousands of people. He has no need to. Propped up in an Empire armchair in the Parisian hotel where he receives a few journalists, his body speaks for him. It is completely paralyzed from the chest down. A group of fanatic Red Guards seized him one evening in 1967. To get him to denounce his father, who had been purged from his position as General Secretary of the Chinese Communist Party and was charged with being the *"second highest leader engaged on the road to capitalism"*, he was locked into a laboratory in the presence of radioactive material. Deng Pufang attempted to escape by climbing along a gutter, but fell from the fourth floor, breaking his spine. The following months were spent in a hotel in Peking without treatment. He was forced to earn his living by making wire baskets for the recovery of soiled toilet paper. During this period his father was carting farmyard manure . . .

Moravia has not died of shame, and the minister of General de Gaulle seeks to return to power. The article I presented in 1975 concluded with the following remarks:

> Bachofen felt that moving from a matriarchy to a patriarchy was equivalent to the subordination of material principles to spiritual principles, the subordination of the chthonic law of the subterranean maternal powers to celestial Olympian law. Psychoanalytic theory does not escape this struggle between maternal and paternal law. If we underestimate the importance of our earliest relations and our cathexis of the maternal imago, this means we allow paternal law to predominate and are in flight from our infantile dependence; if we neglect the organizing effects of the Oedipus complex, which includes the experience of whole objects, of the paternal superego, of the penis, we restore the maternal primal power which, even if it does intimidate us, is an undeniable source of fascination. Our per-

sonal conflicts may cause us to forget that we are all children of men and women.

What strikes me today is how I stressed the *fascination* the primitive mother exerts on the human being; a fascination that can be detected beneath the very immediate and visible fear the archaic Mother inspires. I cannot help thinking that the sociocultural and ideological context in which this paper was written led me, more or less consciously, to examine the other side of the problem. In her existence a woman comes up against the very concrete fact that fear of the primitive Mother prompts men and women to control the female powers and to accord inferior status to the woman. Yet the wish to merge with Mother Nature, to abolish the Ego, to eradicate the father and his attributes and to grasp the cosmic maternal powers, leads men to compete with women, on the grounds that only men are capable of merging into the Great Whole. This rivalry prompts men to envy female powers, to denigrate them and to try to deprive women of them.

In the second chapter, "The Feminity of the Analyst in Professional Practice," I recall, in connection with this issue, that from the genetic point of view, the incestuous object for both sexes is the mother, the womb being our common place of origin. I also say: "It seems to me . . . that her *capacity for motherhood* enables the woman to realize in fantasy her dual incestuous wish: to recover the state of primary fusion with the mother by means of the union established with the fetus during pregnancy, and to keep the love object, the father or his penis, inside herself." In other words, the woman has the extraordinary capacity of becoming one with her mother because of a function that is essentially linked to femaleness. In this chapter I examine the ways in which the femininity of the man as well as that of the woman play a determining role in psychoanalytic practice. However, I consider the psychoanalytic situation as an *analogon* of the Oedipal triangle. The analysand is offered a womb in which to regress, but the psychoanalytic framework is there to set limits to this regression in the same way the father separates the child from its mother.

In the next chapter, "The Submissive Daughter," I deal with a category of female patients whose ties of love with their mothers have been threatened early in their lives. This leads them to maintain a very passive relationship with her, the prototype for which is the condition of the infant, manipulated by its mother. For motives that are linked to their personal stories, these women have failed to integrate their identification with the father in the shape of his main representation, the penis. My hypothesis is that such a psychic structure exists in women who fall victim to sexual murderers, murder being the one way by which they are able to integrate the father's virility. Certain disorders of the thought mechanisms accompany the structure described here.

In the chapter titled "Transference Love in the Male," I examine the case of a patient with important creative capacities who, from the very outset of the analysis, demonstrated a transference love that was both affectionate and sensual. The transference, however, could not develop without anxiety until the patient had passed through a phase within it in which he drew closer to the father figure, activating his homosexual drives. Examination of this case permitted me to understand the paradox of the male Oedipus complex. Transference love for the mother can be more openly expressed once the male feels more secure in his sexual identity, this being obtained through introjection of the paternal penis during the homosexual phase. At the same time, since the subject is more anchored in his male identity, he feels less attracted, less fascinated by a return to his origins and his nostalgia for the lost paradise is less acute—feelings and fantasies which underlie the incestuous wish. The acme of transference love hence marks its impending dissolution.

The chapter "The Archaic Matrix of the Oedipus Complex" seems to me to constitute the heart of this volume. It is also the chapter that motivates me to pursue my study of thought disorders and individual and collective destructiveness. I am not a disciple of W. Bion, and I doubt that anyone would be able to detect his influence in the hypotheses I advance. I do feel, however, that a part of the future of psychoanalysis is linked to the study of thought mechanisms. The reader will have gathered that I consider the paternal dimension of the universe to correspond to a mode of mental functioning that is opposed to the mode reigning in a purely maternal universe—that is, one from which the father, his attributes, his products and his derivatives have been abolished.

I illustrate the theme of the "Archaic Matrix of the Oedipus Complex" by a study of Utopia in the chapter that follows. Utopia is defined as the description of political systems that are proposed as models and built under the sole aegis of rationality (this does not mean "Reason"). I hold that the city dweller, being too far removed from Nature and therefore unable to reach a state of fusion with the mother, is the enemy of Utopias. The Utopian city attempts to resolve this contradiction. I try to show how, drawing my examples from the extraordinary book *We,* written by the Russian dissident Eugene Zamiatine. Is it really mere chance that the first English translator of this book was a psychoanalyst, Gregory Zilboorg? (New York: E.P. Dutton, 1959). My aim is to show how, despite its idyllic facade, Utopia inevitably results in fanaticism, violence and the underlying wish to reach a state of tabula rasa.

The two remaining chapters concern Germany. By way of explanation I should perhaps add that for the past two years I have been Chairman of the Programme Committee of the International Psycho-Analytical Association, whose task it was to prepare the first congress to take place in Germany since 1932. Psychoanalysis is indeed linked to Judaism. Freud was a Jew and most of the first analysts were also Jews. Yet this does not warrant its being labelled as a "Jewish science." For reasons I set forth in "The Paradox of the Freudian Method," the concluding chapter of this volume, Freud's attitude to human phenomena was, however, deeply rooted in Judaism, in the paternal dimension of the Jewish religion and its set of morals. At the same time, German romanticism was an unavowed part of Freud's cultural heritage. German romanticism, more so than any other romantic movement, was dominated by the cult of Nature. Heinrich Heine, as early as 1833, and Thomas Mann in the 1920s, both saw in this cult the signs of a pending apocalyptic catastrophe. Thomas Mann refers clearly and several times to the "maternal chthonian depths" that would come to be celebrated in German romanticism at the expense of reason and moderation, virtues he considered solar and essentially virile (or, as I would term them, "paternal"). Thus, in the most recent of the chapters in this volume, I find that I have returned to the theme I had very briefly outlined at the end of "Freud and Female Sexuality," written ten years before, in 1975.

The second of the chapters relating more specifically to Germany, "The Green Theater," was prompted by the contact I have had over the last two years with Germany and the Germans. The Congress decided to devote one day to the study of the Nazi phenomenon. The psychoanalytic community has been deeply affected by Nazism and this first retrospective encounter to take place in Germany was, I think, a positive event. Mutual fears and concerns, it is true, led to a certain avoidance of the most painful problems, but it is hoped these debates will continue. Nazism and the Holocaust remain the mystery of the twentieth century and have opened up vertiginous glimpses into the depths of the human mind. In this chapter I advance certain hypotheses concerning the forms in which the return of all that the parents or even the grandparents have denied, i.e., their participation in the extermination of the Jews, now manifests itself in German society today, and especially among its young men and women. Once again, the cult of Nature comes to the fore, even if this cult claims to protect a nature that is truly endangered. For Germans too, identification with paternal values is particularly difficult, not only because the father in the personal story has himself fallen into the arms of the *Erlkönig* (whose image is closer to the archaic Mother than to the genital father), but also because of his denial of the past. This prevents the son, or the daughter, from accepting this past as theirs, other than in a projective, persecutory way. The problem of the second or the third generation of Germans is not, in my opinion, that they have no guilt, but that they cannot work it through in a depressive way. Only an integrated form of identification allows one to choose between the characteristics of the object one wishes to keep and to release the energy necessary for the sublimation of the undesirable elements. Faust allied himself with the Devil once he had renounced his father's heritage, his "instruments."

To conclude this introduction, I would like to add that the two trees of Eden (see the epigraph) are not representations of the Mother and the Father, of Man and Woman as such. They are a creation of the mind in the sense that our mental functioning is built after the universal wish to return to the mother's womb and modelled according to the obstacles that thwart this wish and which, to a greater or lesser degree, eventually impel the human being to choose another course and to formulate other wishes.

1.

FREUD AND FEMALE SEXUALITY: THE CONSIDERATION OF SOME BLIND SPOTS IN THE EXPLORATION OF THE "DARK CONTINENT"

Because space is limited it will not be possible for me to deal with Freud's ideas on female sexuality in their entirety, even less to compare them with opposing views expressed by other psychoanalysts. I shall therefore speak about only those issues which have caused the greatest controversy.

Let me open this discussion with a remark of a general nature: if a subject as fundamental as female sexuality causes such disagreement among analysts after almost 80 years of clinical experience, it must be because it stirs up certain internal factors in a particularly intense way which somehow interfere with our progress toward knowledge. Our differences of opinion about female sexuality are such that in the mêlée we lose sight of the truth.

A correlative comment comes to mind: divergencies in our understanding of female sexuality inevitably breed corresponding differences of opinion concerning male sexuality. Bisexuality, the notion of a "complete" Oedipus—both negative and positive—the necessity for dual identification, all conspire to cast the shadow of the "dark continent" onto male sexuality. It seems to me artificial and fallacious to

Presented as part of a Dialogue on "Freud and Female Sexuality" at the 29th International Psycho-Analytical Congress, London, July 1975.

completely abstract the study of female sexuality from that of the femininity common to both sexes and of human sexuality in general.

I shall therefore restrict my study of Freud's work on female sexuality to the discussion of some essential points; but at the same time I find myself forced to broaden the scope of these very same issues.

I shall examine the theory of *sexual phallic monism* and its most important consequences; I shall try to formulate certain hypotheses which I have developed on other occasions, with the idea of showing how Freudian theories of female sexuality have endured in spite of the opposing clinical material which has come to light, in spite of the undeniable contradictions these theories reveal, and finally in spite of those theories which have lent a completely different dimension to female sexuality. I shall express a personal view on these matters, particularly on the topic of penis envy, yet my study will remain very much within a Freudian perspective; my basic assumptions being rooted in the question of "human prematurity," which is linked to the child's early helplessness (*Hilflosigkeit*).

A *Midrash,* a Talmudic commentary, recounts that when a child is born he is endowed with universal knowledge; but an angel appears, touches the newborn's upper lip with his finger and the child's knowledge vanishes into oblivion. It would seem that this legend, which one can imagine as representative of primary repression, is illustrative of theories of infantile sexuality and, in particular, the central one of sexual phallic monism and the correlative ignorance of the vagina, which is shared by both sexes. These theories replace what is probably an innate knowledge. We know, however, that for Freud sexual phallic monism and ignorance of the vagina are not defensive elaborations tied to repression: the vagina is nonexistent for both sexes, *even in the unconscious,* and this lasts until puberty. This postulate is repeated throughout his work, beginning with the *Three Essays* (Freud, 1905); it appears again in "Femininity" (Freud, 1933) and finally in the *Outline* (Freud, 1940). (An important watershed expression of this idea can be found in Freud, 1923). It is noteworthy that in the latter texts Freud is aware of the controversy inspired by the existence of early vaginal desires but he dismisses it abruptly. In "Femininity" he writes (Freud, 1933, p. 118): "It is true that there are a few isolated reports of early vaginal sensations as well, but it could not be easy to distinguish these from sensations in the anus or vestibulum; in any case they cannot play a great part."

In the *Outline* we find in a note Freud's refutation of the "supporters" of the vagina: "The occurrence of early vaginal excitations is often asserted. But it is most probable that what is in question are excitations in the clitoris—that is, in an organ analogous to the penis. This does not invalidate our right to describe the phase as phallic" (Freud, 1940, p. 154).

In his article "Female Sexuality" Freud (1931) answers his opponents on this idea for the first time; his answer is astonishing:

> A man, after all, has only one leading sexual zone, one sexual organ, whereas a woman has two: the vagina—the female organ proper—and the clitoris, which is analogous to the male organ. We believe we are justified in assuming that for many years the vagina is virtually non-existent and possibly does not produce sensations until puberty. It is true that an increasing number of observers report that vaginal impulses are present even in these early years. In women, *therefore* [my italics], the main genital occurrences of childhood must take place in relation to the clitoris (p. 228).

It is obvious that when Freud refutes these theories he takes into account the existence or nonexistence of early vaginal sensations, but he does not recognize that the existence (at least unconscious) of the vagina would completely upset the theory of female sexuality, particularly in our understanding of the female Oedipus complex, of the girl's wish for the paternal penis and the wish to have a child, all of which would become, in this respect, *primary* and fundamentally feminine. The boy child is completely unaware of the vagina's existence and imagines that all human beings possess a penis, including his mother. This is stated plainly in *Three Essays* (Freud, 1905), while at the same time, erections of the penis before puberty and concomitant wishes for penetration are denied. ("The processes at puberty thus establish the primacy of the genital zones; and, in a man, the penis, which has now become capable of erection, presses forward insistently towards the new sexual aim— penetration into a cavity. . . .") In his paper "On the Sexual Theories of Children" Freud (1908) takes into account a number of observations stemming from the case of Little Hans (Freud, 1909). What he describes is quite apropos of what I am trying to say here:

> If children could follow the hints given by the excitation of the penis they would get a little nearer to the solution of their problem. That the baby grows inside the mother's body is obviously not a sufficient explanation. How does it get inside? What starts its development? That the father has

something to do with it seems likely; he says that the baby is *his* baby as well. Again, the penis certainly has a share, too, in these mysterious happenings; the excitation in it which accompanies all these activities of the child's thoughts bears witness to this. Attached to this excitation are impulsions which the child cannot account for—obscure urges to do something violent, to press in, to knock to pieces, to tear open a hole somewhere. But when the child thus seems to be well on the way to postulating the existence of the vagina and to concluding that an incursion of this kind by his father's penis into his mother is the act by means of which the baby is created in his mother's body—at this juncture his enquiry is broken off in helpless perplexity. For standing in its way is his theory that his mother possesses a penis just as a man does, and the existence of the cavity which receives the penis remains undiscovered by him (Freud, 1908, p. 218).

It is noteworthy that later Freud (1924, and especially 1940) pictures the male child wishing only to be near his mother, indulging in vague and imprecise contacts which imply his penis only in an obscure way.

I would like to take up here some aspects of the observations in the Little Hans case (Freud, 1909) which seem to me to contradict the "fuzzy" quality of the excitation of the little boy's penis and to bring into question the entire theory of sexual phallic monism, or rather, to put into very evident relief its essentially defensive nature; thus, simultaneously, we can raise the issue of the equally defensive character of the sexual theories of children in general. We perceive that a complete and intuitive knowledge of sexuality (which is quite unacceptable for many reasons) underlies these theories; this knowledge is complete and intuitive because it is instinctual. How can we possibly imagine the girl to be unaware of the fact that she possesses a vagina when Freud (1917) attributes to the dream the power to discover early on all of the organic changes to come (this is the dream's "diagnostic aptitude")? Why should the unconscious, which possesses the means for awareness of our bodily intimacy, be blocked when it comes to the vagina? Why should the boy not be aware of an organ complementary to his own since Freud postulates elsewhere the existence of innate primary fantasies?

When Hans was three and a half years old, his little sister Hanna was born. His father jotted down in his notebook that day:

At five in the morning, labour began, and Hans's bed was moved into the next room. He woke up there at seven, and, hearing his mother groaning, asked: 'Why's Mummy coughing?' Then, after a pause, 'The stork's coming to-day for certain.' . . . Later on he was taken into the kitchen. He saw the doctor's bag in the front hall and asked: 'What's that?' 'A bag', was the reply. Upon which he declared with conviction: 'The stork's coming to-day.' After the baby's delivery the midwife came into the kitchen and Hans heard her ordering some tea to be made. At this he said: 'I know! Mummy's to have some tea because she's coughing.' He was then called into the bedroom. He did not look at his mother, however, but at the basins and other vessels, filled with blood and water, that were still standing about the room. Pointing to the blood-stained bed-pan, he observed in a surprised voice: 'But blood doesn't come out of *my* widdler.' (Freud, 1909, p. 10).

It seems to me that this excerpt reveals that Hans *knew* that delivery was painful because he was able to link his mother's groaning to the coming of the stork. For certain reasons (he probably felt invaded by those sensations connected to his sadistic feelings and the subsequent feelings of guilt) he still preferred to transform the groans into coughs, which are less worrisome. He also connected, at the same time, the doctor's bag and the arrival of the stork. He therefore knew very well that everything was going to happen inside his mother's body. Moreover, without having been present at the birth, he was aware that the child had come out through the mother's genital organs since he associates his and her "widdler" with the blood.

It should be noted that nothing justifies Freud in assigning to the widdler (*wiwi-macher*) an exclusively male meaning throughout the text; and when Hans asks his mother if she has a widdler too and she answers, 'Of course, why?' (p. 7), it is not necessary to think that she was lying to him because she too possesses genito-urinary organs; Hans's question could be understood as expressing his curiosity concerning the difference between the sexes, of which he was very well aware on a certain level. To demonstrate this idea, let us turn to some of the facts. Just before the outbreak of his phobia he went into his mother's bed in an attempt to seduce her, saying: "Do you know what Aunt M. said? She said: 'He *has* got a dear little thingummy'" (p. 23). Yes, a dear thingummy, but a *little* one. Not a big one like the horses. This was the beginning of a constant theme, the comparison between his *little* penis and the big penises of animals he envied; this provoked in him a fear of horses biting his fingers and a more vague fear with regard to animals possessing obvious phallic traits: the giraffe (because of its long neck), the elephant (because of its trunk), the pelican (because of its bill). Freud writes that Hans's statement, "my widdler will get bigger as I get bigger," allows us to conclude that in the course of his observations Hans never stopped comparing and remained forever unsatisfied with the dimensions of his widdler (and in fact one can imagine that a part of his phobia derived from his wish to steal the big widdlers of the horses and the other phallic animals, which would then come back to threaten him. The fallen horses, the objects of Hans's terror, can be considered, on a certain level, castrated: fallen being the opposite of erect[1]); his wish for a big widdler remained an issue for a long time. Hans's father, like Freud, concluded that Hans feared "that his mother did not like him, because his widdler was not comparable to his father's." The fulfillment of this wish is played out in the fantasy of the plumber coming to give him a big widdler. Where does this wish for a penis as big as the father's originate, if Hans has no idea that his mother possesses an organ that his "dear little thingummy" is incapable of (ful)filling? His knowledge of the mother's vagina appears in two fantasies he tells his father: (1) "I was with you in Schönbrunn where the sheep are; and then we crawled under the ropes, and then we told the policeman at the end of the garden and he grabbed hold of both of us" (p. 40); (2) "I went with you in the train, and we smashed a window and the policeman took us off with him" (p. 41). The idea that his penis is too small for his mother's vagina appears again, I think, in his fear that his mother would drop him during his bath into the big bathtub. That this fear issued from his wish that his mother would drop Hanna during her bath does not invalidate this hypothesis. Like the child who said apropos of the new arrival in his nursery, "the stork should take it away again" (Freud, 1908, p. 212), Hans was just as capable of sending Hanna back where she came from (the mother's vagina). Later Hans talked about the big box (the mother's womb): "Really, Daddy. Do believe me. We got a big box and it was full of babies; they sat in the bath" (Freud, 1909, p. 69). To my mind, this is the vagina.

We cannot fail to recognize in little Hans's fantasies and phobia an *Oedipal wish implying the genital possession of the mother with the help of a penis robbed from his father.*

But what is striking is that Freud sees this too—the material leaves little room for any other interpretation—and yet, in spite of this, he continues to uphold the theory of sexual phallic monism and the accompanying ignorance of the vagina. He says, in fact (Freud, 1909):

Some kind of vague notion was struggling in the child's mind of some-thing he might do with his mother by means of which his taking posses-sion of her would be consummated; for this elusive thought he found certain pictorial representations, which had in common the qualities of being violent and forbidden, and the content of which strikes us as fitting in most remarkably well with the hidden truth. We can only say that they were symbolic phantasies of intercourse . . . (pp. 122–3).

And further:

But this father . . . had been his model . . . his father not only knew where children came from, he actually performed it—the thing that Hans could only obscurely divine. The widdler must have something to do with it, for his own grew excited whenever he thought of these things—and it must be a big widdler too, bigger than Hans's own. If he listened to these pre-monitory sensations he could only suppose that it was a question of some act of violence performed upon his mother, of smashing something, of making an opening into something, of forcing a way into an enclosed space–such were the impulses that he felt stirring within him (pp. 134–5).

At this point, when we think Freud is on the verge of identifying the existence of the vagina at least on the preconscious level in little Hans's psyche, he surprises us with this strange conclusion:

But although the sensations of his penis had put him on the road to postulating a vagina, yet he could not solve the problem, for within his experience no such thing existed as his widdler required. On the contrary, his conviction that his mother possessed a penis just as he did stood in the way of any solution (p. 135).

Freud's conjectures here appear contradictory: firstly, contrary to what he claimed (Freud, 1905) and to what he continued to claim in later works, the boy's wishes for penetration exist well before puberty and so does the "obscure" and "premonitory" existence of the vagina. It would be impossible to prove in any decisive way if at any moment Hans thought that his mother's widdler was a penis, and even so, this repre-sentation would have to be superimposed on that of the vagina. One might ask: if his conviction does indeed stand in the way of any solu-tion, as Freud has written, is this representation then perhaps a defen-sive one—and if this is true, how? One can imagine Freud's answer: the fear of castration would drive the little boy to see a penis where there isn't one. But the fear of castration springing from the sight of the female genital organs without a penis is all the more powerful, according to Freud, precisely because the child is ignorant of the vagina's existence. He therefore imagines a sex not just different from his own, but—horrors!—an absence of sex.

I believe, in fact, that none of these difficulties would arise if, like with the child in the *Midrash,* we considered that little boys and girls were completely knowledgeable about sexuality, but that this knowledge is then tampered with by a series of repressions, of a defensive nature, which result first from the pressure of unbearable excitations, and then afterwards from conflictual situations. (The idea of an "instinctive knowledge" and even an "instinctive patrimony" stemming from the processes of sexual life and constituting the nuclear center of the unconscious was not foreign to Freud, 1918, but he refuses, in my opinion, to draw the logical consequences which necessarily follow. Freud was perhaps afraid that this conception would be exploited for the purposes of Jungian theory.) This would explain why the child shapes his own sexual theories according to his stage of development. The child lives on two planes: that of his profound knowledge, possessed instinctively, of sexuality, and that of his development, his wishes and his defences, which gauge the information the child receives during the course of his growth. Sexual education is therefore caught between two dimensions: the child's unconscious on the one hand, to which nothing can be taught that it does not already know and, on the other, his own sexual theories which he elaborates for his own purposes and which give answer, in principle, to what he feels he can stand at any one stage of his development. When children are informed of sexual matters there is always the possibility that the adult will find himself in Hans's father situation when he said to him (Freud, 1909, p. 95), "but you know quite well boys can't have babies," to which came the reply, "Well, yes. But I believe they can, all the same."

My hypothesis is that the theory of sexual phallic monism corresponds not to the lack of knowledge of the vagina but to a splitting of the ego ("Well, yes. But I believe they can, all the same") *or to the repression of an earlier piece of knowledge.* This hypothesis has already been formulated by Josine Muller, Karen Horney, Melanie Klein and Ernest Jones. However, I hope to put my subject into a different perspective.

Before presenting my hypothesis in full, I would like to discuss another famous clinical text of Freud's, the analysis of the Wolf Man (Freud, 1918). If Little Hans's phobia is focused on the positive

Oedipus, the "infantile neurosis" of the Wolf Man is focused on the negative Oedipus, the wish to *assist the paternal coitus,* to take the mother's place in the primal scene. We know that the child witnessed at the age of one and a half the famous scene of coitus a *tergo* between his parents and that he dreamed his wolf-dream when he was four years old. In Freud's estimate, the reactivation of the primal scene in the dream directed the child toward genital organization, a discovery of the vagina (cf. Freud, 1918, p. 64). This is in contradiction with his theory of the discovery of the vagina in puberty. In a strange way Freud assumes that observing the coitus a *tergo* convinced the child "that castration was the necessary condition of femininity" (p. 78). Our first objection is that in this position the vagina is not visible. Furthermore, we are again faced with the equivocal role the vagina plays in the masculine castration complex, because, in this instance, the vagina is held responsible, above all, for the Wolf Man's castration fears: the vagina is precisely the wound the father leaves after castration. Freud claims, nevertheless, that the child represses his knowledge of the vagina, and adopts instead his first theory of anal sexual intercourse:

> But now came the new event that occurred when he was four years old. What he had learnt in the meantime, the allusions which he had heard to castration, awoke and cast a doubt on the 'cloacal theory'; they brought to his notice the difference between the sexes and the sexual part played by women. In this contingency he behaved as children in general behave when they are given an unwished-for piece of information—whether sexual or of any other kind. He rejected what was new (in our case from motives connected with his fear of castration) and clung fast to what was old. He decided in favour of the intestine and against the vagina. . . . He rejected the new information and clung to the old theory (Freud, 1918, p. 79).

Here again we come across theoretical suggestions that contradict other statements we find elsewhere in his work. Freud (1937) describes passivity, in any form, as sufficient to stir up fears of castration in men; actual penetration is not necessary to awaken these fears of losing the penis. Anal penetration, *a fortiori,* does not prevent man from fearing castration. The fear of passivity, we know, is the "bedrock" of the psychoanalysis of males:

> At no other point in one's analytic work does one suffer more from an oppressive feeling that all one's repeated efforts have been in vain, and

from a suspicion that one has been 'preaching to the winds', than . . .
when one is seeking to convince a man that passive attitude to men does
not always signify castration and that it is indispensable in many relationships in life (Freud, 1937, p. 252).

Furthermore, it is striking that the wishes for penetration by the
father's penis were active in the Wolf Man's case when he observed the
parental coitus (at the age of one and a half) and were revived in his
dream (at four years of age), and yet the same wish for penetration
arises in the girl's case only in puberty. The Wolf Man, like Schreber
(Freud, 1911) wished to have a child by his father, an instinctual wish
tied to his feminine identification, while the girl's wish is only a substitute for, an ersatz version of, her penis envy (Freud, 1925). The man's
feminine wishes to be penetrated and to have babies by the father would
therefore be more direct than the woman's. We should bear in mind that
these wishes constitute for the male individual the nucleus of delusion.

Moreover, we know that Freud (1931, p. 229) asserts in his article
"Female Sexuality": "It is only in the male child that we find the fateful
combination of love for the one parent and simultaneous hatred for the
other as a rival."

Freud considers the pre-Oedipal phase more significant in the
woman's case than in the man's. He claims (Freud, 1931) that sometimes the girl never attains her positive Oedipal phase, and during the
phase of her negative Oedipus complex "a little girl's father is not much
else for her than a troublesome rival" (p. 226). If the girl does reach the
positive Oedipal phase, her relationship to her father is merely a con-
tinuation of the relationship she enjoyed with her mother: "Except for
the change of her love-object, the second phase had scarcely added any
new feature to her erotic life" (p. 225).

If we carry these statements to their logical conclusion, can we not
say that in Freudian theory the father is more of an object for the boy
than for the girl?

Penis envy, in the girl's case, is a derivative of sexual phallic monism.
The Freudian conception implies that from the moment when the girl
discovers the penis's existence, a discovery that antecedes the Oedipal
phase, to the moment in puberty when she discovers the existence of
her vagina, she is, in her own eyes, a castrated individual with a truncated penis: the clitoris. This fact makes her turn away from her mother
who did not offer her a penis and drives her into the Oedipus complex

so as to obtain from her father the desired organ, a desire which in happy circumstances turns into the wish for a child, and preferably a male one. The woman's sexual desire for the penis is absolutely subordinate to or has been flattened out by her narcissistic envy. *Penis envy is primary, the feminine erotic wishes are secondary.*

But, as we all know, the woman's psychosexual trials and tribulations do not end here. Since the little girl's sexuality is in the final account male, and exclusively focused on the clitoris—the external "feminine" genital parts, as Freud significantly calls them, do not come into play at all, even in seduction. Once the girl arrives at puberty she has to give up her cathexis of her "male" organ (the clitoris) and turn toward her internal feminine organs. "What is thus overtaken by repression is a piece of masculine sexuality" (Freud, 1905, p. 221). The clitoris that remains the focus (it should only serve as a transmitter of excitability, "pine shavings" for the kindling of a fire) is at the root of female frigidity and predisposes the subject to the neuroses, most particularly hysteria. Gillespie (1975) poses the following question in relationship to this issue: "Does not Freud's theory of the pseudo-masculine clitoris which has to be given up imply an insistence that the female *must* be castrated . . .?"

We know that the clitoris plays a role for the entire duration of the sexual act and for the duration of a normal woman's lifetime. Jones (1933) implied this when he wrote that "after all, the clitoris is a part of the female genital organs."

I think that we can now list the principal points which have been raised in my discussion of the Freudian theory of female sexuality as it stands in relationship to the theory of sexual phallic monism:

the boy's ignorance of the mother's vagina;
the girl's ignorance of her own vagina;
the girl's exclusive cathexis of the clitoris, the equivalent to a truncated
    penis;
the necessary renunciation of this cathexis at puberty;
the girl's psychosexuality is dominated by the unsatisfiable envy for the
    male organ;
the boy's wish to be penetrated by the father's penis and to have his babies
    is more direct than the girl's;
the positive Oedipal phase is never attained by some women;
the female positive Oedipus complex is only the displacement of the
    woman's relationship to her mother onto her father;
maternity is an "ersatz" masculinity which in fact can never be attained.

Female sexuality is therefore a series of lacks: the lack of a vagina, lack of a penis, lack of a specific sexuality, lack of an adequate erotic object, and finally the lacks implied by her being devoid of any intrinsic feminine qualities which she could cathect directly and by her being forced to give up the clitoris. We can add the relative lack of a superego and the capacity for sublimation, issues which I shall not be able to discuss here. The boy's sexuality is so much more full: he possesses an adequate sexual organ, a sexuality which is specific from the outset, and two love-objects to satisfy the requirements of both tendencies of the Oedipus complex.

Now the woman as she is depicted in Freudian theory is exactly the opposite of the primal maternal imago as it is revealed in the clinical material of both sexes. This could be a mere coincidence, but the contradictions we have been able to discern throughout Freud's work on the problem of sexual phallic monism and its consequences, force us to take closer notice of *this opposition between the woman, as she is described by Freud, and the mother as she is known to the Unconscious.*

What astonishes us in all of this is not that Freud's pathways to knowledge were blocked in certain areas of his work, but that in spite of this he was able to pursue his researches so successfully and so far. The issue is this: this theory still enjoys a solid reputation because, ultimately, it has withstood the contradictions of certain clinical and theoretical arguments, and has withstood the pressure of its own internal contradictions.

The theory of sexual phallic monism (and its derivatives) seems to me to eradicate the narcissistic wound common to all humanity, and springs from the child's helplessness, a helplessness which makes him completely dependent on his mother.

As early as 1895, in *Project* (Freud, 1950) Freud began to place emphasis on the human being's condition of helplessness in infancy, and the situation of dependency it entails. Subsequently (Freud, 1915) he attributes the separation between the ego and non-ego to the infant's helplessness (*Hilflosigkeit*): "the primal narcissistic state would not be able to [develop] if it were not for the fact that every individual passes through a period during which *he is helpless* [my italics] and has to be looked after and during which his pressing needs are satisfied by an external agency . . ." (p. 135, note).

Later, (Freud, 1926) he again mentions the helplessness of the human being, whose intra-uterine existence seems to be short in comparison with that of most animals, and it is sent into the world in a less finished state. As a result, the influence of the real external world upon it is intensified and an early differentiation between the ego and the id is promoted. Moreover, the dangers of the external world have a greater importance for it, so that the value of the object which can alone protect it against them and take the place of its former intra-uterine life is enormously enhanced. The biological factor, then, establishes the earliest situations of danger and creates the need to be loved which will accompany the child through the rest of its life (pp. 154–5).

The human being's dependency on his mother, who is absolutely necessary for his survival, causes for the most part, as we all know, the formation of an omnipotent maternal imago. As the child grows, he gains, through his psycho-physiological maturation and identifications greater and greater freedom. Nevertheless, his psyche remains forever marked by his primary helplessness, especially since it follows hard upon an earlier state of completeness in which every need was automatically satisfied (I am alluding to the fetal state and to the very short period when we can assume that the ego and non-ego are not yet differentiated). Because the child is faced with a discrepancy between his incestuous wishes and his ability to satisfy them, a discrepancy which springs from man's biological chronology—this is a point that Grunberger (1956, 1966) has stressed—the child's experiences of these wishes become a real drama. Here again, helplessness is at the heart of the problem.

Let us remember the bleak picture Freud (1920) paints of the Oedipal child:

> The early efflorescence of infantile sexual life is doomed to extinction because its wishes are incompatible with reality and with the inadequate stage of development the child has reached. The efflorescence comes to an end in the most distressing circumstances and to the accompaniment of the most painful feelings. Loss of love and failure leave behind them a permanent injury to self-regard in the form of a narcissistic scar, which in my opinion, as well as in Marcinowski's . . . , contributes more than anything else to the 'sense of inferiority' which is so common in neurotics. The child's sexual researches, on which limits are imposed by his physical development, lead to no satisfactory conclusion; hence such later complaints as 'I can't accomplish anything; I can't succeed in anything.' The tie of affection, which binds the child as a rule to the parent of the opposite sex, succumbs to disappointment, to a vain expectation of satis-

faction or to jealousy over the birth of a new baby—unmistakable truth of the infidelity of the object of the child's affections. His own attempt to make a baby himself, carried out with tragic seriousness, fails shamefully. The lessening amount of affection he receives, the increasing demands of education, hard words and an occasional punishment—these show him at last the full extent to which he has been scorned (pp. 20–21).

Renunciation of the Oedipal object, in this context, seems to be tied to the child's pained recognition of his smallness, of his insufficiencies. This is the tragedy of lost illusions. The theory of sexual phallic monism maintains these illusions. McDougall (1972) has pointed out that the sight of the female genitalia without a penis not only inspires the child with fright because it confirms the possibility of castration, but it also requires the child to recognize the role of the father's penis and to accept the primal scene.

In my opinion, reality is not only founded in the difference between the sexes, but also in the absolute correlative, the difference between the generations. The reality is not that the mother has been castrated but that she possesses a vagina that the child is utterly unable to (ful)fill. The reality is that the father possesses a penis that the little boy does not have (the big widdler that Little Hans envied), and genital faculties the child does not possess. When the child is forced to heed the difference between the sexes and their complementarity, he simultaneously comes to realize the difference between the generations. *This causes a narcissistic wound that the theory of sexual phallic monism tries to erase:* if in the Oedipal phase the child was devoid of any wishes to penetrate his mother, of any knowledge of his mother's vagina, he would have no reason to envy his father whose capabilities would then be not much different from his own; if his mother were willing, and his father did not object, he too could engage in those vague and imprecise "contacts." The Oedipal boy preserves in this way a measure of his narcissism. In fact, this corresponds to the perverted temptation to render pregenital wishes and satisfactions (within the little boy's reach) equivalent to, or even to value them more highly than genital wishes and satisfactions (which are only within the father's reach). A very clear expression of this temptation is to be found in the analysis of Little Hans, when he states his wish to beat horses and finally, as he confesses, to beat his mother: for a little boy, it is, in fact, easier to do this than to attempt to have genital coitus with an adult woman.

Other narcissistic advantages are contained in the theory of sexual phallic monism: if the mother is without a vagina, the little boy, in terms of the inverted Oedipus complex, can satisfy the father just as much as the mother can. Many homosexuals entertain this fantasy; they believe that the anus, which they have genitalized, and the vagina are equivalent. The supposed lack of knowledge of the vagina offers the male child narcissistic benefits on both the negative and positive planes of the Oedipus complex.

The need for sexual phallic monism finds its origin in two different dimensions of the child's relationship to the mother: on the one hand, the archaic omnipotent mother and on the other, the Oedipal mother; in both instances the child experiences with pain the inadequacy linked to his helplessness. The wish to break away from the primal mother drives children of both sexes to project her power on to the father and his penis, and to more or less decathect specifically maternal qualities and organs. If the relationship to the mother has been a sufficiently good one (for external as well as internal reasons), the male child will choose his father as his model (as in the case of Little Hans) so he can be like him and one day possess his mother. He will then cathect his own penis with an actual sexual and narcissistic value, but one which is to be truly realized only in the future. He will not, however, entirely abandon his narcissistic cathexis of the maternal faculties and organs: breasts, vagina, the possibility of bringing children into the world. This process leads him to develop according to the norms of his own sex, yet without, in a state of reaction, devaluating the feminine elements; he will thus be able to integrate his femininity and increase his capacity to understand the wishes of his partner in love relationships. If his relationship to the archaic mother has been very sour, he can completely remove his narcissistic cathexis from the maternal prerogatives and place it entirely on the paternal penis and his own. Because he will so thoroughly disdain the maternal traits, he will find great difficulty in integrating his femininity, if he does not find it simply impossible. He rejects any resexualization of his passive homosexual impulses; he finds it horrifying. Resexualization is rejected by the ego precisely because the reaction-cathexis of the penis has absorbed the bulk of the narcissistic libido; femininity is thereafter divested of this libidinal content. This would help to explain, in my opinion, the conflicting character of the male's passive homosexual wishes, because the erotism driving the subject toward his father is connected precisely to a devaluation of femininity, and therefore to that of his own. In these cases a violent opposition breaks out between homosexuality and narcissism. I think this is one of the reasons, among the many others cited by other analysts, why with patients revealing paranoid features it is necessary to analyze the maternal relationship early on in treatment.[2]

Freud attributed to man a "natural scorn" for women. This scorn originated in their lack of a penis. My experience has shown me that underlying this scorn one always finds a powerful maternal imago, envied and terrifying (see also Chasseguet-Smirgel, 1964).

A passing devaluation of the mother and women is "normal" and allows the boy to narcissistically cathect his own sexual identity, but it should not be prolonged into adulthood except in the guise of protective feelings toward the woman. Scorn in the adult is never "normal" and reveals personal uncertainty about one's own self-worth. It can be, among other things, the manifestation of a phallic-narcissistic regression. Of course what I said earlier about the defensive nature of the theory of sexual phallic monism does not expel Jones's theses, for instance his thesis on the phallic phase, but contributes to our understanding (at least I hope it does) of the defensive character of that phase that protects the subject not only from his fears of castration on the Oedipal level but also from the narcissistic wound tied to his intrinsic insufficiencies.

In contrast to the subject presenting paranoid symptoms stands the transsexualist who through plastic surgery removes his male characteristics to fabricate a vagina in their place. For precise "historical" reasons linked to his relationship to his parents he was probably unable to project his ego ideal on to his father and his penis. His narcissistic cathexis never detached itself from the maternal feminine attributes of the archaic mother. The male's femininity, his homosexual position are, because of the complex factors we have just described, borne by multiple defensive and instinctual forces:

> classical regression before the Oedipal phase and fear of castration by the father;
> impossibility of identification with a sadistic father;
> "normal" identification with the mother in the primal scene, on the level of the inverted Oedipus complex and the integration of femininity;
> the envious wish to acquire the father's big penis through incorporation, with the goal in mind of paternal identification in the hope of possessing the mother in the positive Oedipus complex;

the wish *to be* the omnipotent mother and to possess her attributes which
continue to be narcissistically cathected (this wish can, consequently, be
perfectly ego-syntonic);

the wish to be the mother so that fusion can occur and separation-anxiety
be avoided;

the wish to be penetrated passively by the mother's anal phallus (I can only
allude to this position here);

the wish to escape the omnipotent mother by decathecting those attributes which belong to her, and by "gluing" oneself to the father and his
penis.

The need to detach oneself from the primal omnipotent mother by
denying her faculties, her organs and her specifically feminine features,
and by investing in the father, seems to be a need both sexes share.
Bachofen (1861) has studied the transformation of matriarchies into
patriarchies. The existence of matriarchal civilizations raises many problems, but Bachofen's work nevertheless touches upon a profound psychological truth, because we can thus observe projected onto the
history of civilizations the individual adventure of development in men
and women.

A psychoanalyst to the end, Bachofen answered Momsen, who had
challenged his theses, that personal reasons must underlie Momsen's
refusal to accept the existence of matriarchies. Bachofen thought that
Aeschylus' *Eumenides* described the transition from matriarchal to patriarchal law. We know that this play is the narrative of Orestes' trial
after he murdered his mother. He had acted to avenge his father,
Agamemnon, who had been assassinated by Clytemnestra. The Erinyes,
who at the end of the play become the Eumenides, are daughters of the
night, chthonian, subterranean divinities who reigned before the time
of Zeus (like the mother who reigns before the father). They are the
prosecutors at the trial. They are described as "the gloomy children of
the night." Apollo, at whose specific command Orestes had set out to
avenge his father, heads the defence. Orestes appeals to Athene, who
was born without maternal involvement; she was born straight from
the head of Zeus, fully armed and helmeted and thus escaped primal
infantile helplessness. She creates a court, the Areopagus, in the very
place where the Amazons had been, before they had been defeated by
Theseus; in this way the Erinyes lose their legal prerogative as judges.
The Erinyes protest:

> Here is overthrow of all
> the young laws, if the claim
> of this matricide shall stand
> good, his crime be sustained.

The Erinyes believe that Clytemnestra's crime is less of an offence than Orestes' because "The man she killed was not of blood congenital." Orestes makes the astonishing retort: "But am I then involved with my mother by blood-bond?" Apollo supports Orestes:

> The mother is no parent of that which is called
> her child, but only nurse of the new-planted seed
> that grows. The parent is he who mounts. A
>   stranger she
> preserves a stranger's seed, if no god interfere.
> I will show you proof of what I have explained.
>   There can
> be a father without any mother. There she stands,
> the living witness, daughter of Olympian Zeus . . .

Athene approves of this speech and claims to be "strongly on [her] father's side." (This conception of birth should be compared to the one Sade postulates on several occasions.) Orestes is acquitted. The Erinyes lament:

> Darkness of Night, our mother, are you here to watch? . . .
> Gods of the younger generation, you have ridden down
> the laws of the elder time, torn them out of my hands

and threaten the country with the worst disaster. The Erinyes are finally promised that they will be made into a cult. They calm down, are made the Eumenides; the play has a happy, festive ending.

It is noteworthy that Athene, a woman, and Apollo, a man, band together to deny the maternal prerogatives.

The girl's penis envy seems to me not to rest upon her ignorance of the vagina and her subsequent feelings of castration (although certain conflicts which arise in this relation almost oblige her to repress her knowledge of this organ; this repression is perhaps normal as has been indicated by Braunschweig and Fain [1971]) but on her need to beat back the maternal power.

I would like to report a session which I mentioned at the last London Congress. I think it very clearly illustrates what I am driving at. I hope that those who are already familiar with this material will forgive me for repeating it here:

> The woman patient was the third in a family of five children. She had two older brothers. A brother and then a sister were born after her. She began the session by complaining about her being with a woman analyst; since women are inferior to men, she was not going to get anything out of being with me (this was a recurring theme). Then she told a dream. She is in a theater. A woman is standing on the stage exposing one breast which is very big, round and swollen. The patient said that the previous day she had read an article about an actress who was in a very special kind of show in Paris in which she would undress in a very obscene way while insulting the public whom she mocked and humiliated. In her dream the patient is in the hall, among the spectators, with her brother and a friend of his. At the actress's feet there is a little 18-month-old boy. At a particular moment the actress throws herself back, lifts up her skirts and reveals her sex. The patient's brother and his friend become very agitated, mock the woman and make a cutting motion with their fingers, a gesture which is aimed at letting her know that she is castrated. The patient continues and relates a fantasy: she could pull on her husband's penis, and his body would empty like a balloon being emptied of its air. It should be noted that she had always felt that her husband was the-son-of-her-mother-in-law, but not a person in his own right. It seems to me that this example very clearly illustrates that underlying her devaluation of the woman (myself in the transference) a very powerful maternal imago is to be found which upsets her status by producing other children after her and by offering them her breast (she was 18 months old when her younger brother was born, the same age as the little boy in the dream). This mother had humiliated her as the actress had done to her public in the day residue. Her resources for overcoming her narcissistic wound were limited, and she chose therefore to indicate the pitfall and failure in the maternal power, i.e., the absence of a penis. It is the only way to triumph over the mother. But to achieve this it is better to be equipped with a penis, like the two young men in her dream who flout their power in the way she could have if she had been the little 18-month-old boy in her dream. In the fantasy that follows the dream, the patient attacks the mother's breast directly by emptying it, the husband's body representing the breast, and his penis the nipple. The husband is then like a deflated balloon, in other words, like a limp breast. On another plane, the husband also represents the little brother whom she castrates and destroys.

My experience with women patients has shown me that penis envy is not an end in itself, but rather the expression of a desire to triumph over the omnipotent primal mother through the possession of the organ the mother lacks, i.e., the penis. Penis envy seems to be as proportionately intense as the maternal imago is powerful.

It goes without saying that the narcissistic decathexis of the maternal organs and qualities which then follow makes identification with the mother and the acceptance of femininity rather difficult. Passive feminine homosexuality is very conflictive and, because of this, integrating it is very problematical. Idealization of the father and his penis perturbs the psychosexual life of women. Athene, the daughter of Zeus, says: "There is no mother anywhere who gave me birth, and, but for the marriage, I am always for the male side with all my heart . . ."

We could pursue in the area of sociocultural activities the undeniable effects of our universal need to escape our primal dependence on the mother, but unfortunately there is no time for that here.

In spite of his views on female sexuality, which reflect, in my opinion, our fundamental conflict with the maternal object as it arises in our state of helplessness in infancy, Freud, because he did recognize the determining force of the child within man, implicitly assigned to the mother the important role that is hers. Bachofen felt that moving from a matriarchy to a patriarchy was equivalent to the subordination of material principles to spiritual principles, the subordination of the chthonic law of subterranean maternal powers to celestial Olympian law. Psychoanalytic theory does not escape this struggle between maternal and paternal law. If we underestimate the importance of our earliest relations and our cathexis of the maternal imago, this means we allow paternal law to predominate and are in flight from our infantile dependence: if we neglect the organizing effects of the Oedipus complex, which includes the experience of whole objects, of the paternal superego, of the penis, we restore the maternal primal power which, even if it does intimidate us, is an undeniable source of fascination. Our personal conflicts may cause us to forget that we are all children of Men and Women.

2.

THE FEMININITY OF
THE ANALYST IN
PROFESSIONAL PRACTICE

The works of contemporary psychoanalysts, such as Kestenberg, for example (1956), which complete and confirm a series of classical works, have, in my view, invalidated and discredited the claims of the theory of phallic monism to be regarded any longer as the gospel truth. In fact, it is not simply a question of rejecting this infantile sexual theory as purely defensive, but of drawing the consequences of this rejection for psychoanalytic theory overall. If the girl stands in the first place not for *deficiency,* but primordially for *receptacle,* then our conceptions of psychosexual evolution must change direction, or even be reversed, and the site of what is most instinctual and animal in the human being must be rediscovered.

I shall do no more than touch upon this vast subject in this chapter, starting from the idea that our vision of human activity must be changed. I mean that the two sexes are marked at the psychic level by the integration of their identifications with their two parents (cf. David, 1975), and identification with a mother, experienced from the beginning as possessing a vagina and a fertile womb, must play a fundamental role in the psychosexuality of men and women.

It seemed to me that it might be interesting, in the context of this Congress, to examine how the femininity of analysts, whether men or women, might affect their professional activity.

The idea of "internal life" and "depth psychology" is associated with femininity; witness the universal symbol of the sea with its echoes of

Presented at the 33rd International Psychoanalytical Congress, Madrid, July 1983.

the genetrix. Fertility is inseparable from internalization, the model for which is probably the penis which is retained to become a child, and not the nipple in the mouth. The proposition is that it is the primacy of the wish for a child, combined with the presence of the feminine receptacle, which produces the oral conception of coitus and pregnancy, and not the primacy of orality over genitality. I will return to this point. Motherhood is consubstantial with female psychosexuality whether or not it results in the birth of a child.

In *Thalassa* (1924), Ferenczi upholds the hypothesis that the return to intra-uterine life constitutes a universal human fantasy and is eventually the biological underpinning of the Oedipal wish. By studying the case of a male patient, I have been able to place the fantasy of draining the mother's insides, which is central to Klein's work, at the heart of the problem. Grunberger (1982) considers it to be the actual expression of basic primary aggression. In my view, this fantasy corresponds to the wish to rediscover a smooth universe without obstacles, roughness or differences, identified with a mother's insides to which one can have free access, the representation, at the thinking level, of a form of unfettered mental functioning with the free circulation of psychic energy. The father, his penis and reality itself must be destroyed in order for the paradise world of the pleasure principle to be regained. It is this fantasy of *the destruction of reality* which confers upon the fantasy of emptying the mother's insides its primordial role. According to my view, it concerns *the archaic matrix of the Oedipus complex* that can be located in the developed Oedipus complex and in the Oedipal myth itself: the murder of Laius at the crossroads (cf. Van der Sterren, 1974) symbolizing the destruction of the obstacle in the way of the mother's body and genitals. In the man, this wish can acquire a more developed meaning in connexion with the Oedipus complex proper. However, on its own and disentangled from its advanced components (love for the mother, admiration of the father, leading to a process of identification), if this wish prefigures the Oedipus complex, it is also its antithesis.

The Oedipus complex is intimately linked with the recognition of differences (between the sexes and between the generations) and reality. It consists of entering into conflict with it, confronting it, not denying or destroying it as such.

As far as the woman is concerned, the wish to rob the mother's insides of their contents can have the same meaning as it has for the man, namely to destroy all the obstacles in the way of a return to the mother's womb. In fact, from the genetic point of view, the true object of incest for both sexes is the mother, the mother's womb being our common place of origin. But we also know that the attack on the mother's womb by the daughter can be the more advanced expression of her rivalry with the mother, the wish to steal the longed-for penis of the father and the babies inside the mother. It seems to me, then, that her *capacity for motherhood* enables the woman to realize in fantasy her dual incestuous wish: to recover the state of primary fusion with the mother by means of the union established with the fetus during pregnancy, and to keep the love object, the father or his penis, inside herself. Thanks to the fusion with the fetus inside her, the woman has the possibility of recovering access to the mother's body in a more complete, more profound and more lasting way than the man. (Here I invert Ferenczi's idea that man might have the possibility of re-entering the mother's body through genital intercourse, whereas the woman could only achieve this indirectly by identification with the man and his penis—and therefore essentially through her own masculine components.)

I would like to emphasize that this relationship to the fetus constitutes a feminine mode of relating to the object, characterized by features including a propensity for more permanent object-ties and a higher rate of monogamy (irrespective of the current fashion): the fetus is, itself, unique. It is probably this possibility of recovering in fantasy access to the mother's body via the capacity for motherhood that accounts for the lower rate of criminality among women, because the obstacles to this wish for a return to primary fusion assume a less absolute form in the light of this option, and consequently the need to remove them by destroying them does not manifest itself in so imperious a fashion.

MATERNAL APTITUDE: THE ANALYTIC SITUATION AND COMMUNICATION

What I will call the analyst's "maternal aptitude" certainly plays an essential role in establishing the analysand in the analytic situation. Ferenczi (1913) showed that the child's environment tends to recreate for him, after his birth, conditions which are as close as possible to the intra-uterine situation: the cradle, soft blankets, cushions, protection from visual and auditory stimuli that are too intense, rocking, soft voices and lullabies all recreate a certain number of characteristics of prenatal life and turn the child's environment into a projection of the womb. It appears, furthermore, that the analytic situation is, in most of its coordinates, in a position to provide the analysand with conditions in many respects analogous with those offered to the infant after his birth, so as to favor a transition from the prenatal dimension of life to its postnatal dimension.

It is reflections of this kind and the study of regression in analysis that have led a certain number of analysts, such as Greenacre (1954) to put the accent on those aspects of the analytic situation which repeat the earliest characteristics of the mother-infant relationship, the back-cloth against which the more advanced conflicts and maturational pro-cesses will make their appearance. For Grunberger (1956), it is the return to the intra-uterine state, to primary narcissism itself, which underlies the analytic situation. From the point of view of our subject, *maternal aptitude* on the analysts' part (in men as well as women) forms the basis of the analytic situation contained within the analytic frame-work, which defines, so to speak, the outline of the womb. But beyond the formal aspects of the couch or armchair, can the analytic rela-tionship itself not be considered a repetition of the mother-infant rela-tionship in its most primitive and immediate aspects, as it is established after birth (to varying degrees, it is true), on the model of the union between mother and fetus? Here we come up against a conflict between two opposing conceptions of analysis: the one in which it is above all an emotional experience, and the one in which it is primarily a verbal communication.

Those who hold the latter view reject, often vehemently, the notion of the "relationship between one unconscious and another" as a way of characterizing, at least in part, the nature of the analytic exchange. Although Freud was little inclined to let his discovery slide into my-sticism, he did not fail to mention, on several occasions, the existence of this kind of communication which is over and above the use of words. Thus in "The disposition to obsessional neurosis" (1913, p. 320) he writes, "But I have had good reason for asserting that everyone pos-sesses in his own unconscious an instrument with which he can inter-pret the utterances of the unconscious in other people." This occurs in fact in the context of a passage concerned with the move by a female patient from anxiety hysteria to obsessional neurosis. The first illness was produced by the frustration of her wish to have children, combined with her husband's sterility. The patient did all she could to prevent her husband from guessing the cause of her difficulties, but, "Her husband understood, without any admission or explanation on her part, what his wife's anxiety meant; he felt hurt, without showing it, and in his turn reacted neurotically by—for the first time—failing in sexual intercourse with her." It was at this point that there was a change in the nature of the patient's illness. I find it interesting that it was in connection with the wish for a child that this exchange took place between one unconscious and another, according to Freud, and I will return to this point.

In "The unconscious" (1915, p. 194) Freud writes, "It is a very remarkable thing that the Unconscious of one human being can react upon that of another, without passing through the Conscious. This deserves closer investigation, especially with a view to finding out whether preconscious activity can be excluded as playing a part in it; but descriptively speaking, the fact is incontestable." In "Two encyclopedia articles" (1923, p. 239) Freud again writes, "Experience soon showed that the attitude which the analytic physician could most advantageously adopt was to surrender himself to his own unconscious mental activity, in a state of *evenly suspended attention,* to avoid so far as possible reflection and the construction of conscious expectations, not to try to fix anything that he heard particularly in his memory, and by these means to catch the drift of the patient's unconscious with his own unconscious." Freud explains, therefore, that the rule of free-floating attention, the counterpart of the fundamental rule of analysis, is intended to provide favorable conditions for communication between unconscious and unconscious. This hidden thread of mysterious communication, is it not the umbilical cord, the prototype of every immediate and absolute relationship? Is it not also their "maternal aptitude" which confers upon both sexes this capacity for preverbal or subverbal exchanges? The regression produced by the analytic situation is experienced by the analyst to a lesser extent, but experienced nevertheless, and it is here that the primitive relationship between the psychic apparatus of the analyst and that of the analysand is established; the primitive relationship which means that a mother can tell the state of her infant at a glance from indicators visible to her alone, and which moreover she could not enumerate. The patient who enabled me to postulate the existence of an archaic matrix of the Oedipus complex, based on the wish to restore access to the mother's smooth inside, dreamed that my street had become a pedestrian walkway (stripped of its obstacles: cars, which were the constant objects of my patient's aggression). A mysterious system enabled us to communicate while I was in my consulting room and he was in the basement of the building, which he identified as a gynecological hospital where he had worked. In my opinion it was a fantasy of a return to the womb where communication between mother and infant takes place in an immediate and total fashion. I am inclined to think that those who refute the existence of communication between one unconscious and another have conflicts in relation to their maternal aptitude, even if a fortunate split enables them nevertheless to make judicious use of it.

I noted a little earlier that it was in the context of the wish for a child that Freud spoke of communication between one unconscious and another. When I thought of personal examples, the first two which came to mind involved the same theme. A patient whose wife was pregnant, began his session by telling me the following dream: "A bull was chasing me and I threw him my red pullover." Before the patient brought his associations, I thought: He wants his wife to have a miscarriage. Then the patient told me that his wife came under the sign of Taurus and that she had presented him with a red pullover. He had had this dream the previous night and had told her about it. (This patient did not usually tell his wife his dreams.) A little later his wife began to bleed. She was taken to a hospital by ambulance. "Fortunately the miscarriage was averted," he said. For some time, in fact, the patient had been talking of stopping his analysis. It was the analytic process which he wanted to abort.

The second example is that of a young colleague, whose schizophrenic patient revealed her pregnancy before she herself knew that she was pregnant.

Cases of communication from unconscious to unconscious extend, of course, to all sorts of situations. However, it seems to me that the predominating theme concerns the wish for a child, the wish to be pregnant, to give birth, to abort. One asks oneself why. If the theory of phallic sexual monism is to be abandoned, if, in both sexes, the representation of the vagina and the active and passive wishes which it excites are simply repressed, if the masculine-feminine antithesis exists from the very beginning, long before the acquisition of the reproductive function, then the wish to make and to have a child also exists, well before the human being has the capacity to satisfy it. It would involve an innate and fundamental wish, which, because it cannot be phys-

iologically satisfied before puberty, is irreparably associated with a narcissistic wound and is therefore destined for repression. The
importance of pregenitality in the human being would be reinforced by
its role as a substitute for genital functioning together with the increase
in ambivalence brought about by this role. The nipple in the mouth,
the feces in the rectum, as well as the teeth in the breast and excrement
accorded the meaning of aggressive weapons would also be pregenital
substitutes for the impossible genital coitus. The attachment of the
sexual instincts to the self-preservative instincts, the later separation of
sexuality on the one hand and life-preserving functions on the other,
with sexual satisfaction being obtained through auto-erotism, all this
could only assume its full force and meaning on account of the fundamental immaturity of the human being which prevented him from being "genital" from the start.

It is important to note that on this point there is a certain lack of
precision in Freud's thinking. Thus, although in *Three essays* (1905)
Freud asserts the accidental and variable nature of the object of the
sexual drive—an assertion which he repeats with some emphasis in
"Instincts and their vicissitudes" (1915), and although he maintains, in
the paper "Femininity" (1933, p. 119) that there is no instinctual attraction between the sexes, "we scarcely know whether we are to believe
seriously in the power of which poets talk so much and with such
enthusiasm but which cannot be further dissected analytically," he says,
it is nevertheless true that he bases his final duality of the instincts on
this force. Thus Eros, sexual instinct and life instinct function on the
model of the union of the gametes: "as regards the sexual instincts . . .
what they are clearly aiming at by every possible means is the coales-
cence of two germ-cells which are differentiated in a particular way"
(1920, p. 44). It is difficult to understand why Freud, in his attempt to
penetrate the ultimate goal of the instinct, accepts that Eros is carried
along by the reproductive instinct, for which there quite clearly exists a
preformed object, and why he rejects the idea of a "natural" attraction
between the sexes in the interests of procreation, an innate attraction, in
my view, which the prematuration period of the human being would
place in a state of latency, seeking substitutes for it, finding satisfaction
wherever it could be obtained, namely through the exercise of the vital
oral and anal functions. If we took this point of view, it seems to me
that we would have a better understanding of the universal presence of
the hysterical core as well as its prevalence in women.

It is clear that, if there is a basic wish for procreation leading to the symbolic realization of this wish, one admits that there is, correspondingly, a genitalization of pregenitality present in hysteria which, as we know, makes use of mainly oral representations to express genital fantasies (the "globus hystericus," for example).

The incorporation of the father's penis in order to make a baby seems to me always apparent in hysterical symptoms based on the model of "container and content," the image of the fetus in the womb. When the hysteric erotizes an organ of the body, or makes the whole body erect, the incorporation of the penis-baby underlies the symptom. The female body, the receptacle for the fetus, is, as we know, erotized much more diffusely than the male body, for the woman is "possessed" in her entirety by maternity, which probably favors the leap from the psychic to the somatic and the capacity to "convert" libidinal energy in parts of her body which are not, *a priori,* erotogenic zones. The "somatic susceptibility" of women may have its origins in their receptivity and maternal aptitude which has no definite boundaries, in contrast to centrifugal male sexuality with its aim of penetration.

It is possible, moreover, to conceive of an asymptotic femininity, as it were, which would be represented by primary identification, all the other modes of incorporation, internalization and identification, demanding the use of elements which could be considered masculine. Whatever the case, female analysands present us, more frequently than men in my view, with material in which incorporation comes *immediately* into operation. This is well represented by the dream in which a female patient found herself in a "funerium." She wondered whether such a word existed. I said, "Funer*a*rium." "Oh yes!" she replied. "When my father died, I acted in a mad, *disgusting* way. I touched his body. I felt it. I couldn't tear myself away from it . . ." "And what became of the *'ra'?*" "I told you yesterday. When I was 3 or 4 years old, my father took me to some seatless toilets. There were rats. [In French the word rats is pronounced 'ra.'] I was *disgusted.* I was afraid to take off my pants . . ." The patient continued and spoke of her disappointment at having been unable to give her father a granddaughter (her daughter was born after his death). Then she brought up her wish to be an analyst. It is clear that the *ra* syllable from funerarium had been literally swallowed, which gives us the key to the dream-wish: namely the incorporation of the father's penis (rat = penis = baby) and of her feelings in the transference.

Because of the fundamental nature of the wish for procreation—

never mind whether it takes us back to the good old reproductive instinct—anything related to the wish for a child, pregnancy, childbirth will become above all else the object of this intuitive, global, immediate knowledge which substitutes for the intra-uterine relationship between mother and child through the umbilical cord. The wish for a child is probably what is least human in man. Remember that Freud in no way rejected the idea of animal knowledge in man: in the Wolf Man (1918, p. 120) he writes, "It is hard to dismiss the view that some sort of hardly definable knowledge, something, as it were, preparatory to an understanding, was at work in the child at the time. We can form no conception of what this may have consisted in; we have nothing at our disposal but the single analogy—and it is an excellent one—of the far-reaching *instinctive* knowledge of animals." Freud considers that this instinctive knowledge forms "*the nucleus of the unconscious*" drawing down to itself "the higher mental processes."

MATERNAL APTITUDE AND COUNTERTRANSFERENCE

Analysts reveal a contradiction when discussing the importance of the sex of the therapist: on the one hand they say that the actual sex plays no part, and on the other hand they recommend analysands undertaking a second analysis to choose a woman or a man (often a woman is expressly recommended when the first analyst was a man).

It is such a common experience that analysands can establish a maternal transference to a man or a paternal transference to a woman, that I will not dwell on this point. This counsel can only be understood, therefore, if one takes account of the analyst's *countertransference,* and assumes that it differs between the two sexes.

I can mention only a limited number of points here with reference to the countertransference and its relationship to the analyst's "maternal aptitude." The first concerns the capacity *to wait* and watch a relationship develop, interpreting it from day to day. A certain number of analysts of both sexes have a brilliant and rapid understanding of the material, but fail in the slow, patient daily labor that is our task. It seems to me once again that it is their femininity which is lacking. In fact, femininity seems to me to be more closely linked with the reality principle, in certain respects, than masculinity. To be sure, gestation requires a certain length of time which scientific progress has not succeeded in shortening. But above all it seems to me that the very essence of the girl's development is dominated by the necessity to wait. Thus, as Klein says (1945): "Together with the unconscious knowledge that she contains potential babies, the little girl has grave doubts as to her future capacities to bear children. On many grounds she feels at a disadvantage in comparison with her mother . . . The little girl in contrast to the boy, whose hope for potency gains strength from the possession of a penis which can be compared with his father's penis—has no means of reassuring herself about her future fertility." I would add that the girl cannot comfort herself with the illusion of being able to become pregnant immediately, unless she becomes deluded, whereas the boy, with the mother as his object, that is to say his primary object, may deceive himself with the aid of his mother into believing that, just as he is, with his little, prepubertal, infertile penis, he constitutes an adequate sexual partner for her, thanks to the splitting of the ego as well as denial of the father's genital universe and all that is associated with it (genital primal scene, vagina, etc.). In other words, the boy can achieve *the compression of time*—and in that case, he becomes a pervert. By contrast, the psychosexuality of the little girl is marked by *postponement*. This factor seems to me to explain, at any rate in part, the lower frequency of the perversions in women. The woman attempts to genitalize pregenitality (hysteria); the man projects his narcissism into pregenitality—in fact onto anality (Chasseguet-Smirgel, 1974, 1978) and, by the denial of genital values, attempts to escape from the paternal universe which gives him a measure of his smallness and inadequacy, for the sexual truth is that only the father (an adult man) can genitally gratify the mother and give her a child.

As I had occasion to describe (1978), perversion is closely associated with sadism and destruction. The woman's "maternal aptitude" accounts, at any rate partly, for the fact that she makes fewer appearances in the field of crime and likewise in that of perversion. In addition, she is, generally and for the same reasons, less inclined to use shortcuts in development, the false pretences that give rise to a whole series of psychopathic disturbances, drug addiction (here, however, we have to take into account her propensity for internalization) and perversions. It is therefore perhaps their femininity which allows analysts to accept the long period of gestation which, at a certain level, analytic treatment represents.

I would like to place the accent on an aspect of the countertransference which is more frequent in men than in women and
inhibits their "maternal aptitude." I have emphasized elsewhere, and in
this chapter too, at least in an allusive way, the fact that the theory of
phallic sexual monism—founded according to Freud on the real ignorance of the existence of the mother's vagina—had a defensive function
in relation to the narcissistic wound which resulted from the sexual
inadequacy of the young male at the age of the Oedipus complex.
However, the denial of the vagina does not seem to me to be exclusively
linked with a feeling of inadequacy (a feeling, moreover, which Horney
elucidated [1932], although she did not relate it to the denial of the
father's genital powers and to perversion). One other motive of this
denial of the vagina results from the fact that the inside of the mother's
body is our place of origin. To admit that the woman possesses an
organ which allows access to her body, is also to uncover the fear of
being absorbed into it, being annihilated by one's return or by being
sucked in by a greedy womb, carrier of the pregenital impulses projected by the subject himself. One of the slips of the tongue which is
most frequently heard in French is the word *mort* (pronounced 'more';
English = 'death') for the word *mère* (pronounced 'mare'; English =
'mother'). Freud's fears about fusion with the mother in oblivion were,
probably, activated at the onset of his cancer. The final duality of the
instincts is often associated with Freud's illness. But his major writings
on femininity are contemporary with the introduction of the death
instinct and carry the undeniable stamp of death. One has only to reread, for example "Some psychical consequences of the anatomical
distinction between the sexes" (1925) to realize that Freud associated
the threat of death which weighed upon him with his ideas on femininity: "The time before me is limited" (p. 249). At this stage of his work,
women and female genitals "the entrance to the former home of all
human beings" are the object of an "uncanny" feeling (1919, p. 245)
and similarly carry the seal of doom. It follows that the countertransference cannot do otherwise than be influenced by such a fear.

The work of Stoller (1968) has enabled us to understand that the fear
of femininity in men has also another source and is linked with the male
anxiety about losing his sexual identity. The young male is, in the
beginning, plunged into the mother's "femaleness." This primary symbiosis must be undone in order that masculine identity can be developed by separating off from maternal identity. This symbiosis, this

attachment, is precisely what the analyst's 'maternal aptitude' runs the risk of failing to loosen. I think that transference interpretations, when given in too insistent a fashion, can have the effect of transmitting to the analysand an unconscious message, in which he is forbidden to invest in objects other than the analyst, and to leave the analytic womb. It is clear that the analyst's "maternal aptitude," his femininity, must also have its limits. Are they not to be found in the analyst's masculinity, in identification with the father, whether the analyst is a man or a woman, which enables the child to cut his tie to his mother and to turn toward reality?

But it is not my aim here to compare the respective roles of masculinity and femininity in analytic work.

To tell the truth, femininity and masculinity never appear in pure form and these two components need each other to manifest themselves. Curiosity, for example, is probably one of the analyst's main qualities (Sharpe, 1930, p. 11) and if it is based on voyeurism and the epistemophilic instinct with their essentially male *penetrating* qualities, does it not also entail the internalization of the object as illustrated in the following material, produced by the patient who dreamed of a "funerium"? I had given her a little card with the dates of my absences in the coming months. One of these absences was on a Friday and Saturday. The patient had said, the following day, that she thought it was "really nice" of me to let her know of my absences on a Saturday and Sunday. Then she realized that I must have given this information to all my analysands, which had disappointed her. I pointed out to her that it was a Friday and Saturday, and that she therefore had wished that I would let her know about my absences when I was with my husband on Sundays. I did not intervene on the subject of the depressive affect which had followed her fantasy. During the following session, she related a "terrible" dream. *She was in a concentration camp with a baby. The baby lost all its teeth. They could be found with a number, 1516. She told this to the camp guard, a Nazi woman, who replied that the child could very well do without its teeth. Then the patient found herself making glasses from teaspoons for children who could not see very well.* It now becomes clearly recognizable that her curiosity induced her to penetrate the primal scene with her eyes and teeth, but also to absorb, to incorporate what she saw, for which she was punished by the Nazi guard. The number 1516 represented the Saturday 15th and the Sunday 16th in her fantasy, since I had given her a Friday 14th and a Saturday 15th as the dates of my absences. (*Quinze cent seize* [Fifteen hundred and sixteen] can sound like '15 *sans* 16' [15 without 16] [as *cent* and *sans* have a similar pronunciation in French] and the Sunday which was the object of the patient's curiosity was thus excluded in order to placate the guard—the sadistic superego—who remained nevertheless inflexible.)

All things considered it seems to me that the analyst's bisexuality must be well integrated to enable the development of the baby made by the analyst and the analysand in their work together, the baby which represents the analysand himself, recreated. Here of course I am looking at it only from the point of view of the analyst.

If I have emphasized the importance of the feminine component and the "maternal aptitude" in the analyst, it is because it constitutes the backcloth to our work, whether we are men or women. It provides the necessary conditions, but does not suffice in itself. In particular, the analytic setting which I recalled at the beginning of this paper as representing the mother's womb is *at the same time* the guarantee that this womb will not swallow up the child, the analysand, forever. As some patients say, the analytic boat has sides which can be grasped in order to get out, and the analytic cot has bars one can hang on to so as not to become lost in a timeless sleep . . . In its role as boundary, the setting is law, a cut-off point, a representative of the father. There exists a dialectic relationship between the setting as the *definition* of a space and the *regression* which it induces and allows, both of which are simultaneously opposed to, and closely bound up with, each other as are the components of human bisexuality. Thus one can consider the patient in the analytic situation as one element in a triangular relationship, corresponding to the schema of the Oedipus complex.

I would like to conclude by presenting a dream I consider to be typical of a woman analyst. It might, moreover, be a recurring dream occurring generally at the beginning of analytic practice. The outline of the dream is as follows:

It is morning. The analyst is arranging her consulting room ready to receive a patient. But her mother, or a substitute, intervenes and by her actions prevents the room from being put in order. The couch is a bed which has to be remade and have a cover put on it, but the mother stays there and, for various reasons, impedes the daughter's work; or else the mother has left some underclothes or her nightdress lying around on the furniture; or else she hangs around in the room and refuses to leave, etc. . . . .

Generally this dream is accompanied by intense rage toward the mother who, it must be said, "is turning the place upside down" when it is time to remove all trace of intimacy of the night and establish the analytic framework. [The French expression for this, *met le bordel,* has sexual connotations not conveyed in the English; i.e., *bordel* = brothel.]

The meaning of the dream is doubtless overdetermined. The dreamer wrecks the analytic framework, and attributes this action to her mother. The wrecking of the framework may be identified with an incestuous relationship with her mother.

The internal mother "inextricably attached to her prey" comes and imposes herself on her daughter as a sexual object in a persecutory fashion. She is the instigator of excitation, prevents desexualization and thus inhibits the functioning of the analyst's thought processes.

At the same time she forestalls the establishment of the analytic framework, thus castrating her daughter of her paternal identification. It is known that women often complain, rightly, that society has prevented the free exercise of the masculine component in their bisexuality, and they hold men responsible for it. I have often noted that behind an intense revolt against men there loomed a violent conflict with the mother. I think that the girl experiences guilt for reasons not only related to her idealized relationship with her father, which I had occasion to describe some time ago (Chasseguet-Smirgel, 1964), but also in connection with escaping from her mother's grasp and primary symbiosis, and assuming the masculine component of her sexuality, the penis being the organ which the real mother lacks and which would enable the daughter, if she had one, to differentiate from her. I think that the dream expresses the conflict and faces us with what is mobilized by the exercise of our profession: the fundamental bisexuality of the human being in its most omnipotent aspects— maternity on the one hand and the legislatory character of the paternal phallus on the other. It is perhaps this omnipotence which, in part, attracts certain people to the profession of analysis. It is also the same force which is liable to give rise to guilt and inhibition. In addition, the two terms of bisexuality are prone to mutual conflict. Could one not therefore suppose that the typical dream which I have just described expresses, at some level, a wild, mad, untamed femininity, boundless and in revolt against its containment within the rigid space of the analytic framework which is identified with paternal law?

However, I would not like to give the impression that I simply identify femininity with what is unlimited, or even impossible to represent and symbolize.

In fact, in this presentation, I put forward the hypothesis according to which femininity was more linked with the reality principle than masculinity. Femininity is paradoxical: it would be the woman's aptitude to find primary fusion again through maternity which would protect her against disorders aiming at short-circuiting the evolution. Man tries, more often than she, to get around and avoid the Oedipus complex. Here, we are confronted with the paradoxical side of masculinity: whereas the father represents the barrier against incest, the obstacle to the merging with the primary object, reality itself (but I have said that reality is above all linked with the little boy's incapacity to satisfy his mother sexually and to give her a child: these are his father's prerogatives), it would be more difficult for the man than for the woman to internalize the father and his phallus with its legislatory character, for he is less able to find again the blessed time when he was one with his mother.

If both sides of bisexuality are in mutual conflict, neither one is a simple element, but, on the contrary, composed of conflicting forces.

The utilization of these components, without any exclusion, is necessary for our work as analysts, whether man or woman.

SUMMARY

The author puts forward the hypothesis that the wishes concerning genitality are present from the beginning, and especially the wish to make or to have a child. From this follows that pregenital sexual satisfactions would be mainly substitutes for genital satisfactions, which are not available because of human fundamental prematurity. Woman's maternal aptitude enables her to fulfil, in displacing it, her dual incestuous wish, i.e., to keep her father's penis inside her during pregnancy, to recover the stage of merging with her mother by means of the fusion with the fetus. This would explain why women are less often murderers than men: an *archaic matrix of the Oedipus complex* would exist which aims at finding an access to the mother's belly, which means to make it perfectly smooth after getting rid of all its contents, that is of all obstacles. This need leads to a destruction of reality. The *disposition to mater-*

nity is common to both sexes (through identification to the mother). The author wants to describe the disposition to maternity of the analyst in the treatment. The analytic situation would correspond to the triangle schema of the Oedipus complex: it favors the regression to the fetal stage, but, at the same time, the *psychoanalytic framework* constitutes a limit which cuts the child from the mother.

3.

SUBMISSIVE DAUGHTERS: HYPOTHESES ON PRIMARY PASSIVITY AND ITS EFFECTS ON THOUGHT MECHANISMS

Yours are the hands which formed me with care, fashioned me into a whole, and you would destroy me! Remember that you moulded me like clay, and you would have me return to dust! Have you not made me liquid as milk, then solid as cheese. You clothed me with skin and flesh, you threaded me through with bone and nerves. You gave me life and mercy, and your watchful care preserved my breath.

Job 10:8–12

It was by chance that two cases that I simultaneously supervised led me to a strange theory. These two patients, both women, appeared to present features similar to those of victims of sexual murder. I can give no proof in support of this, for one woman is, happily, alive; the other died tragically during the course of her analysis, but from an illness with which she had maintained a very curious relationship. At the same time, I had on my couch, a very attractive young woman, part of whose clinical material seems to me to revolve around a dangerous propensity: that of succumbing to a deadly embrace.

These cases have different circumstances: one is a matter of personal experience, the two others have been related to me by two colleagues in training (both women). Of those I have an indirect knowledge outside that unique and privileged relationship between an analyst and her patient.

I shall begin by assembling the material which the three cases seem to me to have in common. It revolves around an "acting-out" which is likely to cause each of these patients to become the victim of a sadistic murderer.

Charlotte is a young woman of 30, who has already undergone a first analysis, the result of which was unsatisfactory. She complains of frequent changes of mood, elation followed by depression, and of an inability to finish tasks she undertakes. When she was first seen at the Centre of Psychoanalytic Treatment she was considered a good prospect for an analytic cure and an excellent supervision case, a diagnosis and prognosis immediately doubtful because the patient presented very marked signs of mechanisms of denial. But when the analyst began to speak to me of it, the treatment had been going on for some weeks and it was no longer possible to reverse it. (I will say now that the organization of these three patients is not identical.) The danger of sexual murder manifests itself in Charlotte in the following manner. She has an eight-year-old daughter from a previous marriage. Her divorce occurred under unclear circumstances. She is living with a man by whom she has a little girl of two and a half. This man, who has quite an important position, is a perverse psychotic who has already spent time in a psychiatric hospital. He will be hospitalized a second time during Charlotte's analysis. He has not had sexual relations with her for a long time. He locks himself in his bedroom to masturbate. One day, Charlotte, in his absence, went into the bedroom and found, pinned to the wall, photos of pieces of the bodies of naked women, cut from pornographic publications. There was not a single photograph of a complete woman. One of her brassieres and a doll belonging to the younger daughter (the one she had had by this man) were lying on the bed. Charlotte's companion several times threatened to kill her and her daughters. These threats alarmed the analyst, and me, when I was told about them. The patient did not seem anxious and at the time was formulating a desire to have a third child by this man.

Caroline is an unmarried woman in her 40s. Behind a vague expectation from life she is crystallizing the (unconscious) desire for a child, stimulated by the departure to Africa of her black lover, with whom she had lived for many years, and who had returned to his native land to take a wife. She had just heard that he had become a father. I referred Caroline to one of my trainees. During her analysis, we learned that Caroline found it easy to pick up a man on the street, and that she would take him home to spend the night with her. One of these encounters had ended in a fight with a woman friend of the man, an Arab. The woman had somehow found her lover at Caroline's house. We were struck by how few precautions Caroline took when choosing partners, and we had expressed the idea, to which I shall return, that she had not internalized the mother as a protector against the danger of castration, a danger which the mother transmits both to the daughter and to the son: "Be careful. Don't go with men who offer you sweets. Don't run too fast, you'll catch cold, etc." It was during the course of the analysis that an episode occurred where the absence of the internalization of a protecting person was obvious. It followed a dream which one could have called a premonition if one did not know the devilish intelligence of unconscious object choices. The dream came after the absence of the analyst for two successive sessions. The patient is telephoned by her mother, who asks her for 200 francs. The patient refuses. The mother then replies: "Drop dead, carrion." This violent and enigmatic dream was unfortunately not interpreted in the transference. In fact, the patient was paying 100 francs a session, and this dream had something to do with the absence of the analyst. On the evening of the second day of the interruption in the sessions, Caroline went to a nightclub and allowed a man to go home with her. When he undressed, she was surprised at the huge scar that crossed his abdomen from top to bottom. He claimed he had been operated on. In the morning (it was a Sunday) the man suggested he go into town to buy food. He dressed, took a string bag, and never returned. Caroline looked in her handbag; 200 francs were missing. From the sideboard where it was usually kept, the table lighter had disappeared. In its place was a large box of sulfur matches; the label had a picture of a vulture.

Carla is my patient. Around 40, she is married and the mother of four children. Carla is a lawyer who specializes in cases involving adolescents. I am her second analyst. She has marital problems that have revived a latent depressive state. The episode that again calls to mind sexual murder happened during her analysis. Carla found herself at 10 P.M. in Paris at the Porte de la Chapelle, alone in her car, which had run out of gas. The area has a bad reputation. She got out of the car to look for a garage. A man came up, asked what she was doing and offered to help. He quickly drew her into a dark street, but suddenly a policeman emerged from the shadows and told the man to clear off. Carla began to protest, saying that he meant her no harm. She realized only at that moment that she had just escaped from some danger, and that the man was either known to the police or had a sinister appearance clear to everyone except her.

When these three cases coalesced in my mind, I wondered what they had in common, apart from the danger to the lives of the women. Certainly it would be interesting to understand the psychic organization of women who are the victims of sexual crimes. I remembered in this context, the case of a lively and merry young woman, a psychoanalyst. She married a psychotic, separated from him and led an independent life but was then found murdered strangled by her stockings. The newspapers spoke of a fiancé she had jilted in adolescence; he had then shot and seriously wounded her, a foreshadowing of the final episode.

We know that sexual crimes also have men (homosexuals) as victims. And if they are linked to femininity, it is as much to that of the man as that of the woman. So, beyond the study of the psychology of the victims of sexual murders, it is to the study of passivity that these cases lead us. And what better description of passivity do we have in psychoanalytic material than that of President D. P. Schreber, a man who, it must be conceded, could only experience it by means of a transsexual delusion? I would like to turn for a moment to *Memoirs of My Nervous Illness,* by President Schreber, so as to extract from it a well-known theme, that of the identification of one's own body with a corpse, the fantasy of ultimate passivity. He writes of a conspiracy whose aim was "to deliver me up to a man . . . while my body, transformed into a female body, . . . would be surrendered to this man, with a view to sexual abuse, in order for it then to be quite simply 'dumped', that is to say, no doubt, left to decompose." He writes further, "I am the first leprous corpse, and I carry around with me a leprous corpse." The miracle of "the putrescence of the belly" leads a part of the soul of von W. to cast "into my belly, with the most consummate brutality, rotting material which causes intestinal putrefaction, so that more than once I thought I must be falling into corruption while still alive, and that the most nauseating corpse-like odour was coming from my mouth," and so on. It would be reasonable to suppose that these anal representations have overdetermined factors. But they are dominated by the fantasy of being completely manipulated "just like a corpse."

"Drop dead, carrion," Caroline's mother said in the dream; Caroline then let herself be stripped by a man-vulture. This patient had, in the same session, complained that the analyst had not properly closed the door at the end of the previous session. One could see her. She made an association with the following recollection: Once she had been to a specialist in the gynecological department of a hospital. She was there, stretched out like meat at the butcher's, with the doctors coming and going as if nothing mattered.

Carla had difficulty using me during the analysis to declare anything that made her suffer, anything that was painful or sad, as if she was at all costs obliged to spare me so that she might be accepted and loved. At the same time I felt that she was as light as a feather during the sessions, which lacked a certain weight—something other patients knew how to impose, sometimes with extreme violence. It was a question of the failure of the mechanisms of projection and projective identification to which I can only refer in passing within this framework. After I had explained the difficulty to her, she had the following dream: "I go to Irina Ionesco's home to get back a carpet which belongs to me. I take it up and roll it. It becomes a roll which I hold upright." Irina Ionesco, Carla associates, is a woman who takes art photographs, actually more like pornographic photographs, of her little girl, whom she shows in poses that are quite obscene, with ostrich feathers, feather boas, lace and high heels. "She uses her daughter for this purpose. I wonder how this child will turn out." (We know that exhibitionism is considered by Freud to be a partial instinct with a passive goal ["Instincts and their Vicissitudes," 1915.]) On the other hand, Carla's husband takes many photographs of his wife. "I get my carpet back . . . You walk on a carpet. Perhaps I don't want to be a doormat any more for people to tread on. An upright carpet—that's phallic, it's better than letting yourself be trampled on. Irina Ionesco is clearly you. There's a big carpet in your office that can be rolled up . . . In my dreams I claim my carpet back." A little while before, Carla had, and for the first time was worried by it, a dream where her passivity was in the foreground: A car wounded her on her hip; she found a strange pleasure in it.

To go beyond these first indications and draw together the elements common to these three women, I am led to state that there is a vital lack of a father. Charlotte's father had been killed in the Resistance when she was one; at her birth her parents were in the process of getting a divorce. Her mother never remarried.

Caroline's father was an itinerant peddler. A Jew from North Africa, he had married a Breton girl who was pregnant with Caroline by him. The Breton mother unceasingly disparaged the father. To give some idea of the depth and special nature of her contempt, I will relate one of the complaints the mother (according to Caroline) had against him. During the war, he had himself baptized, thinking thus to escape racial persecution. The mother used to make fun of him and call him a coward. In addition, she claimed that the father had raped Caroline's sister, then 12 months old! She had proof of it, she said; she took the girl to the doctor at the age of 16 who had diagnosed a venereal disease. As for Caroline herself, the mother claimed she had found her at the age of 18 months making obscene gestures to her father, who was reading pornographic magazines. It should be noted that the patient did not criticize her mother's statements. When her daughters reached adolescence, their mother forbade them to use makeup or to flirt, criticizing any men who would have designs on their virtue.

Charlotte's mother advised her to watch the elder of her daughters, aged eight, closely for, according to her, the child was an object of lust for the caretaker, and was in danger of rape.

It could be supposed that both mothers had an important homosexual kernel, or perhaps were even paranoid, and that they invested their sexual libidos in their daughters rather than in their husbands.

The case of Carla seems at first sight to be somewhat different. Her mother is presented as a forceful woman. The illegitimate child of a woman by her employer, who was an upper-middle-class provincial, she forced her father to recognize her as his daughter when she was 18. Beautiful, intelligent and haughty, she worked at a craft that brought her into contact with people of a superior social class. She made a humble marriage. During the war she played a part in the Resistance. Carla's father was eclipsed by Carla's mother, who is described as fascinating. Without being a true alcoholic, he had a liking for drink. When Carla was nine months old, her brother, aged three, fell seriously ill and was hospitalized for several months. Carla's mother went to see him every day. Afterward she told her little girl that she had been a consolation to her, since she was such a good baby and never made any demands or cried.

Before one of my departures on holiday, Carla had the following dream. She is in the dining room at Baffreval, a boarding school where an adolescent she was professionally concerned with lived. She had her hair done in a great bun on top of her head, tied with pink wool. She associated about my departure and thought that the knot of hair could symbolize a breast. I interpreted her dream by connecting it with the period in her childhood when her mother was apart from her in fact because she was visiting Carla's brother in the hospital and also in thought, since she was then, presumably, completely preoccupied with

her son. By confusing the knot of hair with a breast, Carla was satisfying her desire that I not leave her any more and that the baby (the pink
wool) and the breast become one. In addition, because the breast is so
indissolubly linked to the mother, the dream represented taking possession of the mother's thoughts (the breast becoming a part of her head).
If her intense wish to keep me was being expressed on the level of part-
objects, it was repeating itself at the stage of whole individuals; she was
playing my part in relation to the adolescent she was dealing with in the
dining room at Baffreval.

One can see, among other things in this dream, the importance these
first separations from her mother played in Carla's depression and the
nonexistence of the father at this level.

One remark is indicated here. The three young women of whom I
speak are anything but passive in their everyday lives. They each have a
profession, are thought of as energetic beings by everyone who knows
them, and have active relationships with men. Charlotte fantasized that
she picked up a man and took him to an elegant hotel. We have seen that
Caroline was equally enterprising, yet they are both fairly convinced
feminists. Caroline broke off a relationship that seemed to be heading
toward marriage when her partner asked her to wash his clothes. (One
can see the difficulty there would be in quickly categorizing these
women as "phallic women." One would skirt what was specific in their
psychic organization). As for Carla, she is more discreet. She came to
her sessions at one point with her head full of operatic tunes sung by
men to their lovers. In these women, there was an active, even hyperac-
tive, position, an important homosexual component which manifested
itself, particularly at first, in an attempt to play the part of the father
(absent or inadequate) toward the mother, or to take the place of the
mother's son. This active desire is clearly expressed in the transference.
And yet this activity is only a smokescreen behind which lurks a passivity that is extreme—even deadly.

In thinking about Carla, I hypothesized that this corpselike passivity
was that of the nursling manipulated by its mother. Carla, doubtless
because of the unconscious communication established between the
nursling and the mother, was compelled to reveal nothing of her feelings of distress at the physical and psychical absence of her mother,
which occurred during the illness of her older brother. She was compelled to be the good, happy child, her mother's "ray of sunshine," as
her mother called her.

The two other patients, Charlotte and Caroline, had also both been well-behaved, precocious babies. One might think that these two little girls, both unwanted (since Caroline was the cause of her parents' unhappy and ill-assorted union, and Charlotte was the accidental fruit of a momentary reconciliation between her parents) had had no choice. In order to capture a love that was slipping away and thus to survive psychically, it is necessary, as it were, to be on your guard, to be as good as gold, to reveal neither fear, anguish nor pain. Caroline, was toilet-trained at six months. Even if this claim owes more to legend than to fact, it reflects nonetheless a fantasy of compliance and absolute obedience.

My idea is that the lack of the manifestation of feelings of grief, which are necessary to the maintenance of bonds with the mother, bonds recognized as tenuous and fragile but all the more vital to psychic survival, is accompanied by a proportional distortion of the development of psychic mechanisms and of the sense of reality. In particular, the bad character of the object is denied and the object is idealized. The psychical suffering can only be contained at the price of a transformation in the apprehension of the object itself. Since in all these cases the father is out of the picture, the split between a good and bad object (one of these capable of being projected onto the father) is itself not ensured. Discrimination between the good and the bad is lacking.

Paradoxically, the disinclination to feel distrust for Jack the Ripper, to allow oneself to be struck a mortal blow by him, would be linked to a very early need for survival, at the price of an alteration in the psychic mechanisms, and of a distortion of reality, both threatening to the survival to adulthood.

Opposition to the mother would have come at a later age, as was the case with Caroline, with Charlotte when she was attacked by a mortal illness, and as became true of Carla after a long elaboration during her analysis. But, in any case, the faculty of discrimination had been damaged.

This psychic organization has a bearing on internal as well as external objects. Thus these young women show an astonishing absence of hypochondriacal troubles, and even of fears about health in general. Charlotte's illness serves as an example. One day, she told her analyst that she had had a lump on her breast since the birth of her younger daughter (which had occurred before the analysis began) and that her gynecologist had advised her to have it removed. But, as the doctor had not seemed to think it was urgent, she had not done so. She also had varicose veins and she wondered if she should have the veins or the lump attended to first. It is, no doubt, typical that it should have been I (the supervisor) who was worried about this lump. Perhaps Charlotte's denial was so strong that it involved that of the analyst. You will have guessed that Charlotte had cancer. (I cannot, in the framework of this chapter, elaborate on what made me think that Charlotte had an organization which was likely to lead to a serious illness. I can only seek to unravel what seems to me in this case to have a bearing on the problem on which I have centered my thesis: primary passivity and its effects on thought.) We shall never know whether the gynecologist had herself mistaken the gravity of the illness or whether Charlotte had understood what she wanted to understand: it was only a small lump which would need to be dealt with one day. However, I advised the analyst to try to interpret the careless way in which Charlotte regarded her health, and if that interpretation was unrewarding, to advise her to be re-examined. Charlotte had an operation performed by a surgeon who was in no way a specialist in breast surgery. His intervention, according to a doctor she saw later, made the illness spread. What ensued was a long, drawn-out martyrdom for the patient but also for the analyst, and in her turn, for the supervisor. Charlotte put herself in the hands of a chronobiologist first, and then of a homeopath, her mother's doctor. Every attempt by her analyst to interpret her denial of her illness proved in vain. The cancer spread to her liver in a few months. She went on a holiday to the Club Méditerranée, from where she returned by ambulance to die. For a long time I thought that a profound and strong desire for death had drawn her to an irresistible end. Nevertheless, I wonder today whether it is not still more necessary here to take into account the need, paradoxically more vital than life itself, to deny the existence of the bad object, a need linked to very ancient experiences, which leads to actions that are completely unsuitable because they are anachronistic.

Toward the end of her life, Charlotte had a dream that seemed to me to show a tardy pang of conscience, not only for the sense of unreality with which she regarded her cancer, but also, and more deeply, for the illusion upon which she had constructed her psychic life. That is to say, upon the need for obedience to what she had understood to be a maternal injunction not to show grief, not to protest, to treat things lightly. "My mother gave me some stewed apple. And I thought: All the same, to give stewed apple, to cure cancer . . ." (Of course the meaning of this dream is overdetermined).

Carla for a time showed somatic symptoms which she treated lightly, in spite of their alarming nature. In fact, she was only slightly ill. But most women, in her place, would have been worried. This denial is accompanied by a fixation on bad objects, which are not recognized as such.

Because of this denial Charlotte lived with a perverse psychotic who threatened to kill her and her daughters. Not only did she not leave him, but she repeated in a recurring fashion her desire to have another child by him, as a means of binding herself more closely to him. When she spoke of her lover's behavior, it was her analyst and I who were indignant, not she. During her illness, he never took any interest in her health, never went with her to the doctor, never shared in any of the work which soon became too much for her strength. She never complained. She could not have made fewer claims on him.

Caroline had gone with her black lover on a journey to Africa, his native country. In his country, a woman is generally an object of contempt, and a white woman even more scorned, and she was condemned to walk a few yards behind him. In spite of her declared feminism, she found this normal. This man, who had lived with her for some years, and whom she had helped when he was writing his thesis, had sent her a packet of peanuts for her birthday during the holidays. She found this present wholly suitable because she liked the African method of roasting peanuts.

Carla is certainly the least severely ill of these patients and her analysis enabled her to realize the special bond she had forged with a husband who was brilliant but mentally ill, and from whom she is now separated. It was only during her analysis that she realized her husband's pathological mentality. She suffered from his changes of mood without questioning them, instead considering herself somewhat impatient, even guilty.

Here is one of the dreams she had before their separation. She has to go to André Green (she had read a book by him and he had already been identified in other dreams as my husband, Béla Grunberger: Green = Grün). Green has a house near Giverny (which she associated with my house near the Oise, with that of her parents not far from Giverny and with Monet's paintings of waterlilies). She is in a car with her husband. She is driving. She has the opportunity of parking on the grass, but then she will drown in the water with her husband. She feels something drawing her to let herself slide into the current. (I associate

this with the waterlilies and with Ophelia, which she approves: here she
rediscovers the "strange pleasure" of the wound caused by the car in
another dream previously related). She makes an enormous effort to
park the car in a concrete parking place, where it cannot slip into the
water, and she finally succeeds.

At this point it seems necessary to pose several questions. The first
concerns the Oedipus complex of these young women. There are feeble
remains of a positive Oedipus complex on which it seems to me important to build something to save these women from their tendency to
"let themselves slide," to use Carla's expression, into the arms of Jack
the Ripper (Carla had herself spoken to me of the opera *Lulu* by Alban
Berg, based on the play of Frank Wedekind). In fact, the introjection of
the genital penis of the father seems to me to constitute a safeguard in
the two sexes, against engulfing by the person of the mother. With
regard to the dream of the carpet of Irina Ionesco, I regret not having
evoked the dramatist Eugène Ionesco, even if the pair so formed is
somewhat fanciful; this Eugène Ionesco who drinks like Carla's father.
For these young women, the father is an appendage of the mother, who
must as far as possible be reinstated in his function as an object both
separate and complete, the bearer of a desirable penis.

The active homosexuality which I have said was in the foreground
must not be interpreted as a defense against an underlying passivity. It
represents a more evolved aspect of the relationship with the mother
and bears the signs of an attempted—and healthy—identification with
the father. It also, one might think, conforms to an aspect of the maternal ego ideal adopted by the daughter. It is, finally, and more re-
gressively, an identification with the maternal phallus. So it is that
Carla, taking up the dream of Irina Ionesco again later in her analysis
interpreted it as an identification with the penis of this "perverse
woman" (the rolled-up carpet) and this in relation to an unsuccessful
acting-out which she had had in the metro. She thought she was travel-
ing toward Porte de la Chapelle when she was struck by the notice
forbidding smoking, which was stuck onto the subway map hanging up
in the compartment, and which was in the form of a cigarette canceled
out by two red lines, or "bleeding," as she said. It reminded her in a
flash of the nocturnal incident at Porte de la Chapelle. She then realized that she had actually taken a train in the opposite direction, toward
Mairie d'Issy, which was bringing her closer to me (the nearest metro
station to my home is on this line) and at the same time was distancing

her from the place where the dangerous incident had occurred. She then associated the cigarette with the carpet: both could be rolled. I pointed out that identification with the phallus of the mother is a more evolved position than identification with an object which has no fixed boundaries and which is two-dimensional, such as a carpet or a body floating in the water.[1]

It is equally necessary to emphasize the latent character of this homosexuality and the opposition which exists between my description of these women, who let themselves become involved with Jack the Ripper, and the description of Joyce McDougall (1964) of the fantasies of manifestly homosexual women who fear to be killed by their father or by men in general, who are experienced as sadistic or dangerous. One of the patients described by Joyce McDougall never went out "without a large knife concealed in her handbag to protect herself against the attacks of men with whom she might come into contact."[2] Another of her patients was convinced that a man was going to kill her. She fantasized that her father was sneaking up behind her to cut off her head. We also note that Joyce McDougall establishes the frequency of hypochondriacal fears in women who are manifest homosexuals. According to Joyce McDougall, "the active desire to absorb or to receive anything from the father" is replaced by the feeling "of having to fight off anal and sadistic attacks," and "served as a solid defense against any reawakening of heterosexual needs." In fact, we know that for Joyce McDougall the rejected father has been incorporated, never to be abandoned, in a semimelancholic way. Moreover, the choice of a homosexual object represents a victory over the mother, an attempt to realize independence other than by the normal process of identification, and to supplant her.

On the contrary, the women who I have been discussing, as we have seen, have no fear whatever of men. Not only is the danger denied (I have stressed the absence of discrimination between the good and the bad which seems to dominate their psyche), but it is even unconsciously sought. The mother is there in reality, the object of a relationship of extreme dependence. It is difficult to distinguish traces of the incorporation of the father, whose person is not felt to be dangerous but rather to be insignificant. I have said that he appears like an appendage of the mother or as if engulfed by her. (In Charlotte's case, her father supposedly was shot by the Germans in the train that was taking him to deportation. Indications in her clinical material seem to show that her mother was the railway coach containing the dead father.)

My hypothesis is that women who engage in acting-out in a way that
puts them at risk of being killed by Jack the Ripper have missed out on
the position of manifest homosexuality founded on the possibility of
escaping from the symbiotic relationship with the mother and on the
maintenance of an identification with the father. On the contrary, the
need to keep a bond of love with the mother, a bond which comes under
early threat, impels them to maintain a relationship of passivity with
her, whose model is the state of the nursling manipulated by the mother.
The absence of a lasting introjection of the father and of the paternal
penis (contrary to what happens in the homosexual) reinforces the
recourse to a symbiotic, passive relationship. This cannot, properly
speaking, be described as masochistic. In their sexual lives, these
women are not masochists; their suffering is not eroticized in any special way, not even the passivity itself. It is only after a certain elaboration
of her relationship with her mother in the transference that Carla had
the dream about the wound "with the strange pleasure," and then that
of Ophelia sliding with the current. It is noticeable that in this last
dream, where she escapes from the temptation to deadly passivity, the
third person appears (Green = Grün = my husband). You will note
that this need for passivity reappears after separations. After I have
given her the dates of my absence, Carla thinks I am going to a congress
in Lisbon, about which she has heard. She associates in a session with a
washhouse, with linen, with washerwomen. She imagines herself as
dirty linen in the hands of a washerwoman who rubs, beats and hangs it
out to dry. She thinks of the song "April in Portugal." I remind her that
there is a song called "The Washerwomen of Portugal." It becomes clear
that to be linen in my hands is a way of being delivered up to me so as to
keep me and perhaps be reincorporated in the mother's belly. (I am
thinking of these pictures where water so often appears.)[3]

However, the theme of Jack the Ripper contains something more
than this extreme passivity: it implies, in fact, a deadly penetration. I
have evoked previously the very incomplete nature of the positive
Oedipal situation of these women and their attempt to establish a negative Oedipus complex in which they would play an active part, as father,
brother or phallus. Now these women, as I have said, have not introjected the father's penis, experienced as part of the mother. At the same
time, there is an intense interpsychical struggle against the evolution
toward the positive Oedipus complex, in order to deprive the mother of
the paternal penis which she withholds. The mother, idealized, is the
mother-bearer of the paternal penis, and submission to the mother is, in

the last analysis, submission to an idealized, phallic mother. Now the absence of introjection of the paternal penis produces a void in the Ego, on the two aspects of the Oedipus complex, and one might think that the apparent activity of these women depends above all upon a reaction formation against the underlying temptation of extreme passivity (even if technically it is inappropriate to interpret this to the patients). The passive submission to the mother prohibits the appropriation of the penis which she withholds. Does not then the deadly embrace provide the sole solution for those who would resolve not only submitting oneself lovingly to the mother but also of receiving from her the coveted penis?

The hypothesis I thus put forward brings me to link the problem of extreme passivity no longer merely to its model, common to both sexes, of the nursling in its mother's arms, but to femininity in its receptive aspect. The absence of introjection of the paternal penis is at the root of male homosexuality. We know that male homosexuals can be the victims of crimes which, there is every reason to believe, they have brought about. Doubtless few analysts have had cases of homosexuals capable of being placed in this category. I am aware that it is not a question of simple symmetry, the women of whom I am speaking not being manifest homosexuals. One can nevertheless ask whether, behind the image of the obscene murderer, does not, for both men and women, the idealized image of the mother appear?

Let us recall here the fate of Pier Paolo Pasolini. Dominique Fernandez writes in his book on him, *La Main de l'Ange* (Paris: Grasset, 1982), about Pasolini's mother (he makes Pasolini speak): "and, retaining only from her Catholic upbringing what would feed her maternal instinct, forgetting the Yahweh of Moses as a useless accessory lost in the midst of the clouds, she restricted her religion to the defenceless newborn infant of Bethlehem, to the fugitive from Egypt, to the solitary in the desert, to the abandoned one of Gethsemane, to the prisoner of the Jews, to the crucified one of Golgotha, to he who endured fear and thirst in his agony. Until the day, which was not long in coming, when she herself had a son and could lavish the treasures of her care on a defenceless [*inerme* (Fr.): without the weapon of sting or thorn.] creature: like all Italian mothers, it is true, but, in her case, with the addition of a fervor and an assiduity conferred by the gift of prophecy. I was this son, whom she unconsciously identified with Christ, reserving for herself the role of the Virgin Mary.[4]

Who will pronounce upon the influence of the gospel model upon my secular fate? I did not need to wait for the great trials of Rome, nor the calumny with which the Pharisees overwhelmed me, nor my vile death in a place more desolate than Calvary, to play this role, the first in my century, of a sacrificial victim. Mother had reserved this fate for me from my earliest childhood."

Can one demonstrate with more clarity that the tragic end of Pasolini is inherent in the relationship of the defenceless nursling with his mother, and that the excluded third person—Yahweh the father—will return in reality to pierce him mortally with his dart? Pier Paolo Pasolini died, his arms in the form of a cross, struck down by a blow from a stake, dealt him in a chance encounter with a street Arab.

4.

ON TRANSFERENCE LOVE
IN THE MALE: A "SPECIAL CASE"

My clinical experience (or perhaps I should say, impression) leads me to believe that there are important differences between transference love in men and in women in terms of both its nature and manifestations.

As we know, Freud, when dealing specifically with love transference ("Observations on Transference Love," 1915), considers only the case of women. In Lecture XXVII of the *Introductory Lectures on Psycho-Analysis* (1916–1917), on transference, he mentions cases of affectionate attachment "where there are positively grotesque incongruities, even in elderly *women* [emphasis added] and in relation to grey-bearded men." Here again, he is referring to women.

As we also know, we owe, at least in part, the discovery of psychoanalysis to the passionate feelings of Anna O, which caused Breuer to take flight and induced Freud to recognize the existence of the transference. So is it necessary to be a woman and a hysteric in order to have a love-transference? I utterly repudiate this idea, which, moreover, in spite of certain appearances, I should beware of attributing to Freud himself. No matter: these indications in Freud's work, where he ascribes a more intense and more frequent love-transference to women, can also be linked to his conception of the female Oedipus complex as compared with the male Oedipus complex. According to Freud, the woman "enters the Oedipus situation as though into a haven of refuge" (*New Introductory Lectures* XXXIII, Femininity, 1933, p. 129). Being ignorant of castration anxiety, she does not feel herself to be threatened in her integrity by her mother; on the contrary, having been born incomplete, she rushes into the arms of her father to obtain from him the penis which she lacks ("Some psychical consequences of the anatomical distinction between the sexes," 1925). I have never accepted this elegant asymmetry without reservations. Similarly, I shall not put down the differences which I observe between women's and men's transference love to the account of the classical Freudian theory.

The features that generally characterize male transference love seem to me to be as follows:

1. It is much more camouflaged than in women. While Freud noted the character of *resistance* which transference love may assume in women (preferring living and feeling to understanding, losing sight of the aims of the analysis), it seems that in men resistance *through* the love-transference is less common than resistance *to* the love-transference.

2. Where the love-transference is fully "overt," it is intensely sexualized and lacking in affectionate elements; the incestuous fantasies are sometimes conscious, giving a picture which culminates in perversion. I would not call this a love-transference in the strict sense but rather a sexual transference.

3. *Resistance to the love-transference* induces the analysand to seek refuge in oral and in particular anal pregenital components and the aggressiveness attached to them.

4. *Idealization* of the analyst, in the positive Oedipus situation (toward the mother) is rarer than in women (toward the father). If it exists, the erotic aspects are powerfully repressed and undergo anticathexis. The affectionate current is separated from the sensual current.

In other words, the complete picture of transference love, coinciding with that of the state of being in love as described by Freud (*Group Psychology and the Analysis of the Ego* [1921], Chapter VIII: Being in Love and Hypnosis) — projection of the ego ideal on to the object, not impeding eroticism and accompanied by affectionate feelings — seems to me to be rare in the transference manifestations of male patients — at any rate, rarer than in women.

It was the existence of such a transference in a patient whom I shall call Norbert (N for neurotic, and as an allusion to Norbert Hanold, whose passion for Gradiva is a typical example of love-transference, although not experienced in the analytical situation) which enabled me to understand better the reasons for this difference between the sexes.

Norbert came to see me when, at the age of 27, he was seized with paroxysmal anxiety states, associated in general with fears of diseases liable to affect his genitals. He was sufficiently well-versed in analysis to regard his symptoms as "sickly caricatures of the castration complex." I shall select from his material only the elements which are closely connected with my subject; this is obviously artificial, but is inevitable.

In the preliminary interview he mentioned the recent retirement of his father, who had occupied a very high position in the French civil service; this retirement had been marked by an impressive ceremony. He himself had, to his great surprise, just passed a difficult examination in his particular field of science. (He was in fact to prove an extremely brilliant subject, creative and capable of research and discovery at a high level; these potentialities were to flower as a result of the analysis.) It was therefore Oedipal guilt that brought Norbert to analysis, just at the point when he was climbing the ladder of success his father was in the process of coming down again.

It was not long before Norbert brought in the elements of a (maternal) love-transference. He dreamt that we were setting off by car to Italy. His association was with a honeymoon. He also dreamt that I invited him to tea; I brought the tea on a tray which was in fact his mother's which came from the east, whence her family originated. Soon after the beginning of the analysis I had to change the time of one of his sessions. He dreamt that the couch was rickety and, the same night, that he was to meet me at a country house. The session was to take place. It was evening and he had missed the last train back. He did not know what happened afterward; the dream ended there. Or perhaps it did not. It was the next day. There was sunshine, trees; the countryside was beautiful.

I should like to note here that every time I had to change the time of a session for reasons beyond my control, these dreams of the wobbly couch recurred, or else he dreamt of Dali's "limp watches." In another dream his mother is angry and someone recommends she buy a watch in Switzerland. He was frequently to have a recurring dream at the same time, but also at times other than when I had to change his appointment. He visits a museum of Greek antiquities and a "crazy" woman acts as his guide. He flies to America and the pilot of his airplane is sometimes drunk, sometimes mad. These dreams, of course, represent his view of the analysis and the analyst as putting him in danger, but in a *specific* way, to which I shall return. His mother is represented as an affectionate but restless and terribly seductive woman, asking her sons (Norbert is the eldest of three boys) to zip up her dress, moving about in front of them scantily dressed, while the father is a stern man of striking appearance, proud and commanding. According to Norbert, his father had always had a contemptuous, harsh and unfair attitude toward him. Norbert felt aggressive toward him but obviously admired him. His attacks quickly became bolder, taking on definite elements of castration in the transference. For example, he dreamt of General de Gaulle sitting in an armchair moving on wheels. His symptoms (fear of various diseases) appear as obviously connected with his Oedipal conflict. For instance, at a time when he was getting on in his work and expecting to pass a further examination, he dreamed that he had been invited to an imposing public building, a university. In an office with the door open sat a supreme assembly of men of august and severe appearance, ready to welcome him as one of their own. He was to enter "the high spheres," a term he had used to refer to the milieu of his father. But at the threshold of the office he stopped; he was intimidated and afraid to step forward.

The next day he arrived for his session out of breath. He had had difficulty in climbing the stairs. Perhaps he had a muscular disease? Something in his legs . . . He had had a dream. A superb apartment. A suite [*enfilade*] of rooms, each more sumptuous than its predecessor. He passed through them filled with amazement. There was a reception, an abundance of exquisite dishes, flowers, a luxurious atmosphere. Something that reminded him of my flat and the private residence of Gwendoline (a former mistress). He stopped suddenly and asked, "What was I talking about yesterday? A dream? Whatever was it?" The analyst answered, "You were afraid to step forward." I hardly need to say that his fear was of entering his father's "high spheres" and that these represent the mother's body — that of the analyst in the transference. The word *enfilade* has a sexual connotation in French. If he penetrated the mother's body, so full of wonders, his legs (penis) would be paralyzed. The transference was becoming specific and assuming a form with an aspect of overwhelming passion which this dream conveys:

"We are in the mountains, in a cable car above snow-covered peaks. The telpher breaks away and we join hands. It is an endless fall and great happiness."

In the next session Norbert told me that when we said goodbye, my handshake reminded him of the hand of the Commendatore's statue in Mozart's epic *Don Giovanni* — immediate punishment by the paternal super-ego for the feelings experienced in the dream of the contact with my hands, showing how easily Norbert could move from the mother transference to the father transference in one and the same session. This mobility seems to me to indicate that the patient is firmly anchored in his identity. In my view, deeply regressed patients, unsure of their sexual identity, are the ones who tend most to cling desperately to the *reality of the analyst's sex,* who have the most resistance to using the analyst as a transference object of the imagos of the two sexes and who, above all, find it difficult to accept interpretations given to them of these male projections onto a woman (for reasons relevant to our subject, it is certainly relatively easy to accept the projection of the mother imago onto a male analyst). (I owe a debt here to Stoller regarding the importance attributed to the establishment of male identity. But he does not subscribe to the "ethological" theory of the imprinting of the mother's "womanliness" on the child.)

Another of Norbert's dreams brings out the romantic, affectionate and sensual character of the transference:

"I go into your consulting room. Instead of the curtain rods [*tringles*], there are hawthorn [*aubépine*] branches which are deliciously scented.[1] We go toward the couch. There is an atmosphere of happiness and plenitude."

The next thing to emerge was a memory of "rape and violence" associated with his father. When Norbert was small, he hated cooked endives. One day, when he must have been about four years old, his mother had made some and Norbert had refused to touch them. His father took him to the toilet and forced him to swallow them over the WC seat.

This memory did not seem to me at this point to have been experienced in the father transference but rather as an appeal to the mother to protect him from the father.

After the emergence of this memory, other aspects of the mother imago were to come to the fore for a prolonged period. Not only had she been cruelly unfaithful, producing in turn two small brothers for Norbert (his relationship with his brothers was a theme which underwent considerable working-through in the analysis), but also her seductiveness was absolutely unbearable. If he were to turn to his father to escape from this seduction, this would also be dangerous: his father raped him by forcing the despised endives down his throat. Yielding to this seduction would expose him to the threat of castration, as his symptoms and material indicated, but also to *another danger,* as became obvious in the transference.

Norbert called his anxiety states "the bitch" (this word has less of a sexual connotation in French than in English). They had in fact practically disappeared after one year of analysis. One day he told me a dream: "Two rival gangs were shooting at each other. It was an exchange of bullets. [The French word *balles* can mean either bullets or balls.] Eventually someone is hit." I said: "The match between Pecci and Borg." (It was at the time of the Davis Cup.) Norbert was silent for a moment and then continued as if stricken: "Yes, you're right . . . the little brown-haired South American [Norbert has brown hair] against the title-holder. My father is Danish, of Scandinavian origin, like Borg . . . How did you guess that the only match that I watched on TV was that one? That frightens me . . . *The bitch comes back.* If you can read my thoughts like this, then you and I have become a single person. It is a complete fusion. I am afraid. You see, the bitch is like that picture you have there. A sort of disturbing being, a man or a woman, a monster, hair or a beard. You don't know any more. The bitch comes back." (The picture showed a kind of Neptune composed of dried plants and lichens.) I then pointed out to Norbert that we talk of a "bitch on heat." Was this not what he wanted to tell me when describing to me his mother's seductiveness, restlessness and volubility? Norbert concurred. Would this seductiveness not be all the more disturbing because it constituted in his fantasy a threat of loss of his personality, both as a man and as a separate being? And if I could guess his thoughts without his having to express them, did this not mean that I had already swallowed him up? Would we not then form a monster like a couple making love, in which it was no longer possible to distinguish what belonged to the woman and what to the man? This reference to the combined parents in the primal scene seemed to me technically important. I felt it necessary to introduce the figure of the father into this indistinct amalgam. However, I remain uncertain as to the priority of the imago of the combined parents over the representation of the reincorporation by the mother of her product, the child, the primitive matrix of incestuous fantasies. Is it not this fantasy which lends its specific color to the imago of the combined parents enjoying mutual oral, anal and genital satisfaction and arousing the child's sadism, the anxiety of mutual destruction, particularly that of the father, swallowed up by the mother in coitus — in both sexes. The child then projects onto the parental coitus his or her own desires and fears of being reabsorbed by the womb, and the *incestuous fantasy of the positive Oedipus complex is confused in boys with a return to their place of origin*. This return threatens the boy just as much in his male identity as in his identity in general, much more so than the incest in the positive Oedipus complex of the daughter, who is not lost in the father's body. The penis represents as it were a stop, which protects from symbiosis, from the melting of the boundaries between the ego and the non-ego, and from death.[2] And the *horror of incest* to which Freud refers is associated, in men, not only with the fear of castration or, as I have tried to establish following other authors,[3] with the disproportion between the little boy of Oedipal age and his mother, an adult woman, who can be satisfied only by the big fecundating penis of the father, but also with the fear of losing his identity and, what forms its basis, maleness, in a return to the place from which we all stem, "the former home of all human beings,"[4] the mother's womb. Surely the permanent mutual satisfaction of the parents in the imago of the combined parents is nothing but a repetition at all levels, including the genital level, of the fantasy, or rather, perhaps, of the biological and psychical trace of the permanent and total gratification of the fetus inside the mother's body. Paradise lost and the threat of loss of ego, eternal satisfaction and death, fascination and horror.

One day Norbert arrived for his session and was asked to wait in the sitting room by the receptionist. I was late for reasons beyond my control and, after apologizing for the delay and offering to Norbert to make up the lost minutes, I began the session. The bitch had returned. It became clear that this attack on the established order (the time of the session) had been experienced as an attempt on my part at seduction. If the framework became unstable, everything became possible and incest was imminent. After the event, I understood the floating, rickety, broken, smashed-up couches which appeared in Norbert's dreams after my (infrequent) time changes as indications that the analytical framework itself was, as it were, a materialized representation of the incest barrier. While the "crazy" museum guides and the drunken or mad pilots represented the analysis and its dangers in general, they also principally represented what subsumed them all: terror of the fatal attraction of incest.

That the pilot always took Norbert to America, the adored continent, the "promised land" as he put it, where, in reality, on every trip, he felt intense jubilation on landing is a further indication of the incestuous character of the analytical journey for him.

At the same time, homosexual themes surfaced increasingly boldly. For a long time, this homosexuality emerged without any apparent worry in connection with "fraternal" objects, of the same generation as the analysand. One day, however, Norbert dreamt that he was eating a delicious fish. The analyst featured in the dream. His association was with a biological experiment he was performing at the time on fish sperm. I put this dream together with the episode of the endives which his father had forced him to swallow, suggesting that what he described as a terrible rape might also contain an idea of pleasure.

Norbert—who usually understood everything—was on this occasion impervious to my suggestion and came to the next session with the following dream: There was a nuclear war. The Russians were coming. He and his family were in hiding and it was vital to see that one of his brothers entered the Resistance! I showed him that the idea of sexual pleasure enjoyed with his father was as terrifying to him as a nuclear war and invasion by the enemy, and that my comment about this pleasure must have been experienced by him as if I were myself forcing him to swallow the endives, causing a part of him to feel it to be vital to go into resistance. In fact, the working through of his homosexuality extended over about two years. In the first months of this working through, the paroxysmal anxiety states returned, affecting his body and literally forcing him into analytical laboratories and doctors' consulting rooms. Norbert was afraid in particular of the effects of the (real) radioactivity which existed at his place of work—this was associated with the nuclear radiation in the dream recounted above. Another dream showed that the fears of homosexuality were themselves permeated and nourished by the fears of retaliation for the death wishes connected with the positive Oedipus complex: A friend of his parents, a powerful and revered man, had just died. In his dream, Norbert was beside his grave and was trying to protect himself with a shield from radiation emitted by the corpse, which threatened to contaminate him. (An underlying fantasy could be detected here: pregnancy = tumour: the father's child.) What was clear in the transference was that Norbert had gone into resistance for a considerable time. He missed sessions, arrived late, etc. This was a long way from the magic of the love transference. He was caught between the Scylla of being swallowed up by the mother and the Charybdis of "atomization" by the father. He had a dream whose first part he described as horrible and whose second part as sublime, which showed that at this point in his analysis Norbert had gone so far as to seek refuge in his mother's arms against the mortal embrace of the father:

He had gone to Franck et Fils, a smart fashion shop where his mother liked to buy clothes for herself when he was small. There he was forced to swallow some poison and commit suicide. It was terribly frightening. Then the scene changed completely. He was still at Franck et Fils, but it was at the same time an extraordinary confectioner's shop. There was Lanvin chocolate. A beautiful, gentle, ardent woman came toward him. A perfect sexual union took place between them. This was the opposite of the previous part of the dream.

Norbert produced associations to this dream for a number of sessions. The poison reminded him of the endives. The Lanvin chocolate put him in mind of an advertisement where Salvador Dali said on television, "I am mad about Lanvin." I reminded him that he had often spoken to me about a portrait of Freud by Dali which I had in my consulting room. He concurred. We could now see how the woman-mother-analyst was offering him her body and all her favors (the breast) in order to dispatch the image of the father and his endives (the poisoned penis), but that the problem in this dream remained that which connected it with his father (Franck et Fils [Franck and Son]).

Here the transference love in the positive Oedipus complex is visibly used as a protection and defence against the negative Oedipus complex. Nevertheless, it was sensual and affectionate impulses genuinely present in Norbert that served this end.

Norbert was certainly struggling in his negative Oedipus complex and was not short of ingenious solutions. He had an admired superior at work whom I shall call Dupond-Durant. Norbert dreamt that he was in a car with him. "We were driving over a flyover, you know," he said, "one of those structures that shortens your journey by avoiding crossroads, difficulties and traffic jams. At this point Dupond-Durant said to me: 'What if I were to screw you, that would be funny, wouldn't it?' This is the first time I have had such a crude dream. Dupond-Durant is a double-barreled name . . . [like the analyst's]. I had no anxiety in this dream, it was as if the homosexuality was unimportant. It is nothing but a joke." The analyst responded, "An unimportant joke, a way of avoiding the weight of things, and their seriousness, like the flyover which lets you step over obstacles, and jump over what would give rise to anxiety in the analysis."

Finally, I should like to recount another of Norbert's dreams which features the same person; he had the dream about two months after the one discussed above:

"I have had a fabulous dream. An extraordinary voyage in a boat. *It was a meeting with the sea.* The usual dimensions had burst their bounds. It was the Pacific. Dupond-Durant was there with his children. In reality they have been touring America. He was explaining everything to them. The sea creatures, absolutely sublime; the crustaceans, magnificent. There was a dimension of freedom, hugeness and adventure. Strange, the presence of Dupond-Durant. It is an allusion to homosexuality. You know, the dream in which he said: 'That would be funny, if I were to screw you . . .' There was an atmosphere of escape, that's the word I was looking for, escaping from the jaws of a vice. Freedom, the sea . . ."

About a month and a half later, Norbert, who had already mentioned the end of his analysis, remembered his dream and wondered whether the ocean did not represent life without analysis. He then thought of a dream his brother had told him. He could not remember the dream any more. Oh yes, it was about his analyst. His brother had finished his analysis about a year earlier. Norbert asked him whether he still analyzed his dreams. He had said, "Yes and no." "Shall I forget you or not? Will you forget me or not?"

The ocean dream seems to me to represent the integration of homosexuality in the transference. The penis of Dupond-Durant, the father-analyst, the one who explains and who "screws" (*enfile* [this word also legitimately means "threading"]), is introjected. This introjection confirms Norbert in his masculine identity. He can now *go to meet his mother*. In French "sea" (*mer*) and "mother" (*mère*) are pronounced the same way. She no longer presents the danger of swallowing him up and melting down the boundaries of his ego. The transference love in the positive Oedipus complex blossoms forth in its splendor, force and violence. However, I suspected that its aesthetic qualities still perhaps corresponded to the relics of a secret terror.[5] Be that as it may, it seems clear enough to me that it was the permanence of the introjection of the father's penis in the transference that Norbert was considering when thinking of life without analysis, alone before the ocean, alone before the force of his incestuous desires which drag him toward the mother.

So Norbert embarked on his analysis with a transference love whose object was the mother. This transference love was manifested directly with the full complement of its sensual and affectionate components and with the idealization proper to the state of being in love, which, however, did not constitute an obstacle to the expression of sexuality. This was possible only because Norbert, a neurotic patient on the genital-Oedipal level, was relatively sure of his male sexual identity.

The first manifestations of Norbert's love-transference, however genuine they were, lacked a dimension which was given to them subsequently by the introjection of the father's penis. It is this introjection that allows Norbert to "(truly) meet the sea," asserting himself fully toward it in his maleness. This introjection will probably also turn him away from his mother by putting an end (however relative) to the fascination of the return to his origins and the nostalgia of the paradise lost. What I am saying here could be understood as a description of the institution of the evolved superego, which according to Freud is the heir to the (male) Oedipus complex and gives rise to the renunciation of incestuous love.

However, it seems to me that I am distancing myself in certain respects from these classical views. For what Norbert's material shows is, in my opinion, that beyond castration anxiety and infantile inadequacy, what gives rise to the dissolution of the Oedipus complex *at the same time* constitutes that which brought it to its full flowering. This apogee is connected with the introjection of the genital penis of the father. But once the male identification with the father is well established, if the boy is no longer terrified of fusion with the mother, he has less reason to feel nostalgic for it — is he not now sufficiently distinct and separate from her to turn to other objects? This is surely also a powerful reason for the dissolution of the Oedipus complex. After all, if castration anxiety (persecutory fear for the ego) were all that were involved in the renunciation of the mother, could a "normal" resolution of the Oedipal conflict even be imagined?

In the analysis, the introjection of the analytical framework = barrier against incest = father's penis, also performs this function. And as we know, the analyst's attitude is a part of this framework. Thus, on the day I agreed to Norbert's plan to terminate the analysis, he said to me: "You know, I always felt that the day would come when we would fall into each other's arms. I thought that analysis was the place where all desires would be fulfilled. It's mad to think that, isn't it? In fact you have always been kind but neutral. My passion was 'forward' [he said the word in English] and not 'backward.' I am thinking of Baudelaire's poem . . . "Le Sphinx" ["The Sphinx"] . . . No, "La Beauté" ["Beauty"]." He recited the first four lines of this poem:

Je suis belle, ô mortels, comme un rêve de pierre.
Et mon sein où chacun s'est meurtri tour à tour
Est fait pour inspirer au poète un amour
Eternel et muet, ainsi que la matière.

I am beautiful, o ye mortals, like a dream of stone.
And my breast, where each has tormented himself in turn,
Is made to inspire in the poet a love
Eternal and mute, like matter.

"The dream of stone . . . The stone breast . . . I love shy women. I shall have to mourn for this passion. Homosexuality is easy now. I've taken that in hand. But this fire, it will have to be put out."

I believe that this breast contains the father's penis. And if the stone hand of the statue of the Commendatore (the superego) appeared as a persecuting penis, the stone breast represents this protective "stop" which allows the incestuous passion to be confronted and at the same time finally makes it possible to cathect the other love objects life offers.

It is possible that the importance of the introjection of the paternal penis — the basis for the identification with the father and for the acquisition of a male identity — confers on masculine sexuality and interests that particularly strong measure of homosexuality of which women so often complain. This phase, difficult to integrate, constitutes a fixation point which leads men, more often than women, to separate the affectionate current and the aim-inhibited instincts from the sensual current, by splitting the love object. This love object is split less often into "the mother and the prostitute" than split according to sex, the current formed of aim-inhibited instincts (generally, in my opinion, not sublimated, that is, containing an important amount of simply re-pressed libido) being directed toward men and the sensual current toward women. From whence arise the reproaches of women who think men consider them as merely sexual objects (woman regarded as a thing). It is equally possible that the obstacles which this introjection finds placed in its way (fears for the ego, fears for the object) lead a number of men to behave as if they possessed a genital penis, with the aid of either its substitute or its prefiguration: the anal-sadistic penis. If women, by reason of their frequent idealization of the father, a fact which I have had occasion to stress in the past (1964), repress and counter-cathect their anality, men, on the contrary, seek to defend themselves against their incestuous desires by activating their anality, which protects them from merging with the mother and anchors them firmly in a pseudo-masculinity.

I have stressed (1985) that in perversion the subject regresses to the anal-sadistic stage, which constitutes an imitation or parody of the genital universe of the father. I here quote several lines which supported the development of my thesis. The anal-sadistic universe "appears in the history of the development of an individual as a rough draft or a preliminary sketch of genitality. It is only later in life that it becomes an imitation of it. Freud's article, 'On Transformations of Instinct, as Exemplified in Anal Eroticism' (1917) throws light on this subject." The anal-sadistic stage appears "not only as a specific mode of pregenital organization, but as a kind of protogenitality or of pseudo-genitality in which objects, erotogenic zones and gratifications are adapted to the limitations of the prepubertal infant with the small, unfruitful penis, which is not the case with objects, erotogenic zones and gratifications of a genital nature. According to Freud the fecal 'stick' foreshadows the genital penis; the production of feces becomes a prototype of birth (the infantile sexual theory of childbirth through the anus). The daily parting with the feces is a precursor of castration; the excrement in the rectum anticipates genital coitus. If, in the course of development, the anal-sadistic phase appears as a kind of 'trial gallop' for the child on the way to adult genitality, an attempt to replace genitality by the stage that normally precedes it is a challenge thrown down to reality. It is an attempt to pass off an organized world of pretences as reality. The 'Planet of the Apes' has taken the place of the world of humans."

Nevertheless, the "monkey business," which, to my mind, culminates in perversion, constitutes a masculine temptation, which spreads even beyond the perverse organization (a temptation from which Norbert for the most part escapes; but he is, as I have emphasized, at a level of development which is rarely attained). Indeed, the possession of an anal-sadistic penis permits the escape from a certain number of conflicts linked to the (painful) difference between the mother and the child. That the child's small, prepubertal penis is not capable of fulfilling the mother brings with it the desire to take possession of the large, fruitful penis of the father, in order to identify with him, together with the problems that this position produces. He may well be tempted to endorse features and objects of the anal-sadistic phase,[6] like contempt, indifference toward the object, strength, cruelty; all of which bestow on our civilization many of its most detestable features as well as false emblems of masculinity, faceless bureaucracy, violence, torture, the jackboot and the whip — pseudomanly values of a society which possesses only an illusory show of patriarchal authority.

5.

THE ARCHAIC MATRIX OF
THE OEDIPUS COMPLEX

My work with perverse patients has convinced me of the existence of an archaic matrix of the Oedipus complex which I would like to distinguish from "the early stages of the Oedipal conflict" of Melanie Klein.

In order to develop my idea of this primitive core of the Oedipus complex, I shall refer here to the clinical material of patients, parts of which material have already been presented in another context. We know that, for Melanie Klein, "the sadistic phantasies directed against the inside of the (maternal) body constitute the first and basic relation to the outside world and to reality. The child expects to find within the mother a) the father's penis b) excrement, and c) children . . . According to the child's earliest phantasies (or 'sexual theories') of parental coitus, the father's penis (or his whole body) becomes incorporated in the mother during the act."[1] Klein clearly establishes that there is an equivalence between the external world and the mother's body ("The sadistic appropriation and exploration of the mother's body and of the outside world [the mother's body is an extended sense] . . .") and between reality and the mother's body ("In the earliest reality of the child it is no exaggeration to say that the world is a breast and a belly which is filled with dangerous objects, dangerous because of the child's own impulse to attack them").[2]

Klein confirms this equivalence between the exterior world, reality and the mother's body. But she clearly postulates a previous stage where the mother's breast represents the first object. "In proportion as his sadistic instincts increase and in imagination he takes possession of the interior of the mother's body, that part of the body comes to represent

Ballard Lecture, 11 December 1984, Columbia University, New York.

the whole person as object and symbolizes at once the external world and reality. In the beginning, it was certainly the mother's breast which represented for the child the external world, but now the interior of her body, which is the image of the object and of the surrounding world, takes on a wider meaning, since it has become, because of the extension of anxiety, the receptacle of an increasing number of objects."[3]

We have then, from Melanie Klein, a theory which gives a central position to the fantasy of destroying or appropriating the contents of the mother's belly, and this in an impulse in which the author recognizes elements connected with the positive and negative Oedipus complex, acting precociously, and under pressure from oral frustrations. It is a question of a genetic theory, with a precise date: Oedipal tendencies occur in the second half of the first year of life, and it is the interior of the mother's body which becomes the stage for the expression of these instincts, and no longer the breast, which is the object of oral instincts.

Now, if we turn to Freud, we find, paradoxically, in his work *Inhibitions, Symptoms and Anxiety* (1926) the elements of a theory which would give to the Oedipus complex a core which is less genetic and more structural. It is in the conception of anxiety that this theory of the Oedipus complex seems to me to be outlined. The Freudian theory of anxiety of 1926 is well known, so I will summarize it only briefly.

Anxiety made its first appearance as a reaction to a state of danger. It has for its foundation an increase in the sum of excitation which provokes unpleasure, as well as actions to relieve this tension.

A historical experience, the prototype of anxiety, is the trauma of birth. One remembers that if Rank's book[4] here gives Freud cause to reflect, Freud had himself established the link between birth and anxiety starting in 1909 with *The Interpretation of Dreams,* a hypothesis repeated in 1917 in *Introduction to Psychoanalysis* and in 1923 in "The Ego and the Id." The baby, at birth, is overwhelmed by excitations, that are a source of unpleasure. The corresponding affect is an *automatic anxiety.* The anxiety will arise again during the absence of the object (the mother or her substitute), to an extent whereby this absence is the source of a situation of danger, provokes a need that gives rise to an increase of tension, and therefore to excitations and unpleasure: thus the absence of the object means the absence of satisfaction. "The content of the danger it fears," says Freud, "is displaced from the economic situation on to the condition which determined that situation, viz., the loss of object."[5] The status of anxiety changes and it becomes an alarm signal. "What happens is that the child's biological situation as a foetus is replaced for it by a psychical object relation to its mother," (p. 138), which allows for an absolute and immediate satisfaction of its needs. All anxiety situations can be linked to separation anxieties. Castration anxiety in the phallic phase is the danger "of being separated from one's genitals. Ferenczi[6] has traced, quite correctly, I think, a clear line of connections between this fear and the fears contained in the earlier situations of danger. The high degree of narcissistic value which the penis possesses can appeal to the fact that the organ is a guarantee to its owner that he can once more be united with his mother—that is, to a substitute for her—in the act of copulation. Being deprived of it amounts to a renewed separation from her."[7] So there are connecting links between the primary anxiety of birth and the castration anxiety proper to the Oedipal phallic phase, between the incestuous fantasy and the wish to return to the mother's womb: the central thesis of Ferenczi in *Thalassa* is here adopted by Freud. Two years before publishing *Inhibitions, Symptoms and Anxiety,* Freud had sent to the members of the Committee the famous circular letter of February 15, 1924, in which he discussed the recent work of Ferenczi and Rank. Referring to Rank's *The Trauma of Birth,* he says, among other things, "We have known, of course, for a long time, of the fantasy of the mother's womb, but, from the position that Rank gives it, it takes on a much more important signification and reveals to us, at a stroke, the biological background to the Oedipus Complex. If you connect the ideas of Ferenczi with the views of Rank, Ferenczi's idea according to which man can be represented by his genitals, you have for the first time the derivation of the normal sexual instinct which fits in with our understanding of the world."

Freud, in this letter, distances himself from Rank's conception, according to which anxiety concerning incest would only be a repetition of the anxiety of birth. In *Inhibitions, Symptoms and Anxiety* Freud, on the contrary, links castration anxiety with the anxiety of never being able to return to the mother's body. In the 1924 letter, he already connects the wish to return to the mother's womb with the incestuous wish. At the same time, the father, an obstacle to this two-fold desire, becomes identified with reality. Freud writes, "Obstacles, which evoke anxiety, the barriers against incest, are opposed to the phantastic return to the womb: now where do these come from? Their representative is evidently the father, reality, the authority which does not permit incest."[8]

The hypothesis I would put forward is that there exists a primary desire to discover a universe without obstacles, without roughness or differences, entirely smooth, identified with a mother's belly stripped of its contents, an interior to which one has free access. Behind the fantasy of destroying or appropriating the father's penis, the children and the feces inside the mother's body, a fantasy brought out by Melanie Klein, and, according to her, specific to the early stages of the Oedipus conflict, can be detected a more basic and more archaic wish, of which the return to the smooth maternal belly is the representation. It is a question of rediscovering, on the level of thought, a mental functioning without hindrances, with pyschic energy flowing freely. The father, his penis, the children represent reality. They have to be destroyed so that the mode of mental functioning proper to the pleasure principle may be recovered. The fantasy of destroying reality confers on the fantasy of emptying the mother's belly its primordial role. It is the contents of the belly which are equivalent to reality, and not the container itself. The empty container represents the unfettered pleasure. Dreams of slipping and of flight are not only dreams of erection (they are, moreover, common to both sexes); if they signify the orgasm, it is only to the extent that the subject moves unchecked in a space which is smooth, similar to the fantasy of the empty and completely accessible mother's belly. The reality is that the mother's belly is not freely accessible. All the obstacles on the way to the mother's belly represent reality. Béla Grunberger, in "Narcissus and Anubis" (1983), puts forward the hypothesis of the existence of an immediate aggression born of the collapse of the happiness of the prenatal paradise.

THE DESTRUCTION OF THE CONTENTS
OF THE MOTHER'S BELLY SEEN AS
THE DESTRUCTION OF REALITY

One of my patients, whom I shall call Romain, passed part of his life in quarrels with motorists. He dreamed that my street had become a pedestrian precinct, thus stripped of its obstacles—cars and their drivers—objects of his constant hatred. A mysterious system allowed us to communicate with each other, I from my office and he from the basement of the building, a place he identified with a gynecological hospital where he had worked.

It seems to me that this dream shows very well that it is a question of ridding the interior of my body of its undesirable contents (the cars) and of coming back into my womb (the street, which has become smooth, and the basement, which is identified with the gynecological hospital). We thus established an immediate and complete communication, similar to that existing between the fetus and its mother. Generally speaking, this patient was unable to tolerate obstacles placed in his way. For example, one day when I had made him wait several minutes, as he stretched himself on the couch he said, with restrained fury "You don't have the right to do this. This is my time. I want to get into women's bellies and take out everything they have inside them."

Another of my patients, whom I shall call Alexander, had a series of dreams in which I or his mother were made barren. Ordinary enough dreams, certainly. What was less ordinary was the absence of guilt that went with them and the excitation that greeted their interpretation. Here is an example of one of them: "I am mowing a lawn. I throw the grass into a river. This grass pollutes the waters in such a way that it destoys the fauna and the flora forever. Then I see a mass of jelly. Maybe a small calf." The patient's desire to make his mother sterile is then interpreted in order to show the analysand that this desire endangered the analytical process itself. The patient entirely agrees with this interpretation. He goes on about the calf as a fetus and his mother's miscarriage. Then he associates with the excitation he feels when he imagines having intercourse with a woman with shaven genitals, a fact he associates with the genitals of little girls and with those of his sister, with whom he had very often had sexual games when a child. To mow the lawn means therefore to make the maternal genitals smooth and to deprive her of her secondary sexual characteristics, which are proof of her capacity to contain children and to give birth. The smooth genitals of the mother therefore echo the desire to make her belly accessible.

The same patient also had a dream in which his father-in-law underwent an operation and had his penis removed. In its place there was a smooth surface. Here the smooth genital of the paternal figure is equally a guarantee of the smoothness of the maternal belly, which will contain neither penis nor child.

Romain, and another patient showing a similar perverse organization (to which I shall return), had in reality carried out several abortions, from motives which, they said, were due to their "ideals."

Alexander had the following dream after I told him that the fee for a session was missing in the amount of money he had given me: "I go into a dissecting room and dissect the body of my wife [Alexander is a doctor]. With a scalpel, I lay bare the thigh to the bone. I ask for a saw to cut through the femur. I fuck the corpse." He goes on: "I have sexual needs but my wife doesn't. There is no give and take; she doesn't depend on me sexually. That must be my mother: someone on whom I was dependent. I do not understand my wife, I don't understand that we don't get anything out of being together. I reproach her for being as cold as a corpse. The thigh, it's a symbol of sexuality. I try to extract the femur which is inside. My wife's attitude exasperates me. When I was little, I could not bear not to be taken seriously. I dreamed of my mistress. She had tiny genitals like those of a little girl.

"Is it because my wife resists me, and because my mother belonged to my father? Do I want to get revenge? Has it got anything to do with pregnancy? To open up the belly, to terminate a pregnancy . . ."

That day I did not interpret anything to the patient. I need not say that a neurotic patient would not have had this dream or would have had it in a form of a nightmare. He would surely not have so easily perceived the mother under the image of his wife.

In the following session, the patient came back with fantasies of persecution, aiming thereby to fight against the depressive affects that he expressed, not in the form of real guilt, but in a lowered self-esteem. He claimed, "You are making a martyr out of me. I am being killed by you." I showed him that he was projecting onto me what he, in the dream, makes his mother suffer, so he can take revenge on her for his not being the only one, the undivided favorite (the patient used to say he was his mother's favorite). The femur . . . Before I can finish, the patient says it is his father's penis. Then he adds that life it not worth living. I connect this affect with the fact that I have asked him to pay for a session—the missing fee probably representing the father's femur-penis which he is withholding from me—and that my claim is for him proof that I do not love him unconditionally, for no return.

The patient continues: "At the judo club I don't pay anything, just because it's me. The thigh, it is not free; you say about a woman that she is easy game; that's why I associated with my mother, who used to laugh at the customer's jokes [his parents kept a small café]. I must cut out my guilt." I showed him that his guilt persecutes him as if, now, the father's penis-femur "cut out" from his mother's body had penetrated him to destroy him. He replies that he is not as he would have liked to be, "not an ideal person. I saw a television program about incest. All my life I've chased after something unobtainable . . ."

The dream of a young woman who had a homosexual relationship and who consulted me because of depression shows a similar wish. This dream took place after some months of analysis. The transference is dominated by aggressive feelings against me as a mother who does not fulfill the daughter's demand to be the only beloved child of a woman having no man in her life. All the rivalry between her and her two sisters, respectively 2 and 4 years younger, is reactivated because her youngest sister, whom she admires, loves and hates, has just begun a very successful career as an actress. This sister is also the mistress of a well-known producer. The dream takes place before the Easter holidays—an interruption of the analysis—with underlying fantasies of my having intercourse with my husband, taking care of my children, giving birth to new babies, etc.

Here is the dream: The whole earth has been turned topsy-turvy. Everybody has disappeared except for 34,000 people. [Afterwards she associates this figure with the monthy cost of her analysis.] The earth has returned to the Ice Age. I, and some of the people who have remained alive, are in a sled on a road leading around the world. It's a wonderful feeling, exhilarating, somewhat idyllic. "We felt enthusiastic. It was like skiing on soft smooth snow."

On the same night she had another dream, which she reported in the same session. Her former lover, Lewis, wants to meet her family, especially her mother. They mount a staircase. When they are at the top, they see the sea beneath. He tries to let her fall into the sea. She is frightened, but attracted. At this moment she sees her mother. Then the scenery changes. Somebody is totally submerged in the water in a bathtub. She wonders how it is possible to breathe [the return to the state of a fetus]. Then they are in a church. There is a priest, but it is not a church mass. It is a black mass. She is sitting with one of her legs on the altar. This is in Montparnasse, where her sister lives with her lover, the producer, she adds; she associates with the ceremony she had to accomplish when she was a "fresher," standing nude in front of the audience and miming intercourse with another first-year student.

Without going into the details of this dream, I think that here, in the destruction of all obstacles (the catastrophe which brings the world to an end, leaving the patient alone with the 34,000 people representing the analyst, who is one with Mother Earth and is now completely accessible: one can ride on a sled all the way around experiencing a wonderful feeling of exhilaration), one can distinguish the wish to return to the smooth belly of the mother analyst. The homosexuality represents a means of returning to this fetal state, as the rest of the dream shows: the lover who wished her to fall into the sea doubtless represents the masculine part of herself which penetrates the mother to become a fetus again, the person submerged in the bath. Finally, the black mass and the ragging ceremony point to the meaning of the perverse act as such: going back in the reverse direction along the road that leads from indifferentiation to the evolution toward maturity, from the state of the fetus to individuation.

The same patient told me, this time before the summer holidays, that she thought she was my last patient. I asked her why. Her reply was, because you are old and you are certainly going to retire. She is in fact expressing the wish that she would be my last child, and is attacking me in my maternal, creative capacity. After the holidays the attacks resumed. My place, she said, "smells of old age," exactly like her grandmother's house. Not that it smells bad, but it just smells "old." Then she evoked the wards where elderly, incontinent people are hospitalized, and her grandmother, who was deranged. There was neither rhyme nor reason to what the grandmother said. She used to see things. She didn't think "straight." The patient was very attached to her grandmother, especially after her grandfather's death, when she had her all to herself.

Here I wish to emphasize the way in which the patient set out to attack my thought processes. She identified me with her grandmother, whom she wanted to have all to herself but prior to examining the fundamental problem of the attack on the processes of thought, I suggest that thought in itself constitutes an obstacle which prevents access to the smooth maternal belly and that its statute is analogous to the statute of the father and his derivatives: the penis and children.

In a more general way, I feel that the material I have just reported shows very well that the destruction of the contents of the mother's belly, aiming to make it smooth and perfectly accessible, represents the destruction of reality itself. Reality is, as I have emphasized, that the father and his fruitful penis alone are capable of satisfying the mother, which is not the case with the prepubertal and infertile penis of the little boy, whatever may be the illusion under which the mother has sought to keep the child. To express this at a deeper level, it is possible to conceive of reality as being made up of differences. Rather than to speak of the difference between the sexes and the generations as representing the only bedrock of reality, it would be more appropriate to think of reality as being entirely the result of differences. Time, for example, can be thought of as an interval between the need (or the desire) and its satisfaction. Space implies that one takes into account the difference in situation of the points composing it. Reality is made up of a crosssing over from a state of homogeneity to one of heterogeneity. This leads one to examine the desire to empty the mother's belly of its contents (which is to retrace in an opposite direction the path between homogeneity and heterogeneity) as giving concrete form to the struggle between the pleasure principle and the reality principle.

THE ARCHAIC MATRIX OF THE OEDIPUS COMPLEX CONSIDERED AS AN OBJECTIVIZATION OF THE STRUGGLE BETWEEN THE PLEASURE PRINCIPLE AND THE REALITY PRINCIPLE

A dream by Romain, the patient who used to quarrel with motorists, seems to me to illustrate very well what I intend to put forward: "A fish is exhibited with its mouth open. You can see the inside of the body, which is smooth. We bet that we can throw a pebble into its mouth, and that it will roll right down to the anus and come out. Then the fish's mouth puckers up and changes into a vagina. It retracts. The vagina and the anus are now one and the same thing. Then it becomes something like a snake-penis. Right beside, there is an exhibition about the Jewish people. There stands X, toward whom I feel homosexually attracted. From time to time, people have to climb up onto stepladders. In fact, we are in a gas chamber."

I ask the patient what link there is between the fish story and the exhibition. He answers that "anything can be done with either of them. The fish changes into a mouth, a penis, a vagina and an anus. Soap and lampshades were made out of the Jews."

The smooth, completely even aspect of the fish's inside is notable. It is the image of an object, as well as of a world, in which the impulse runs clean through, and where there are no differences between the parts of the body, which are no longer separated, and change one into the other. A universe submitted to the total abolition of the limits between the objects and even between their molecules, a universe which has become totally malleable ("anything can be done . . ."). This universe without obstacles, this smooth maternal belly, is also a fatherless universe, where the subject confers upon himself the Creator's powers, thanks to anal production (common to man, woman, child and adult), which is in opposition to genital procreation (the prerogative of the father). I will return later to the anal character of the scene. However, it seems necessary for me to insist that the subject succeeds in again finding a way of functioning proper to the pleasure principle, that of seeking satisfaction by the shortest and the quickest route, without detours or postponements. This is well brought out in the bet that the pebble thrown into the fish's mouth will travel through the body until emerging from its anus, according to the tendency of free energy to circulate without hindrance. What seems to me especially interesting in the dream is that, in a way, the mental functioning according to the laws of the primary processes, proper to the pleasure principle, *is itself so represented*. The dream does not only fulfil a wish by methods which are typical; the wish which is dramatized and fulfilled here is, precisely, that of *a mental functioning according to the pleasure principle*—that of the dream itself.

In "Formulations on the Two Principles of Mental Functioning" (1911), Freud introduces the activity of thinking as an important stage in the acquisition of the reality principle. "A new function was now allotted to motor discharge, which, under the dominance of the pleasure principle, had served as a means of unburdening the mental apparatus of accretions of stimuli, and which had carried out this task by sending innervations into the interior of the body (leading to expressive movements and the play of features and to manifestations of affect). Motor discharge was now employed in the appropriate alteration of reality; it was converted into *action*.

"Restraint upon motor discharge (upon action) which then became necessary, was provided by means of the processes of *thinking,* which was developed from the presentation of ideas. Thinking was endowed with characteristics which made it possible for the mental apparatus to tolerate an increased tension of stimulus, while the process of discharge was postponed." Freud adds that the action of thinking is accompanied by a transformation of free-flowing cathexes into bound cathexes. Thought, therefore, made its appearance in order to serve the reality principle, even if a part of the activity of thinking can be detached from the reality testing and remains under the control of the pleasure principle (fantasizing, daydreaming).

It seems to me that the declaration of war that a certain type of patient (particularly the pervert) makes against thought is caused by the bonds which thought maintains with the reality principle. A dream of Romain, the man with the smooth fish, seems to me to bear witness to this: "I am breaking walnuts with my bare hands. I feel as if I should not do it. They are fragile, and I am not skillful enough. *I put them into a melting pot.* I was struck when awoken that walnuts looked exactly like brains. At the same time, the swollen nutshell makes me think of a woman's belly."

This patient had earlier had a long dream in which the same melting pot appeared, full of diverse things, including paper and a pen, representing a supposed activity of the analyst taking notes about the dreamer, as well as a ruler and a man's shoe. All these things were going to melt, like pieces of cheese, into an undifferentiated mass, or like pieces of meat being grilled, all alike, in "a Burgundian fondue" (the patient's words).

So it is a question of destroying thought, the brain, the tools which help the analyst to think, the paternal penis, the ruler (the rules), the fetus—the whole contents of the mother's belly. Notice that the patient considers the brain and the fetus to be identical, both being obstacles which have to be made homogeneous, reduced in order to become an undifferentiated mass. In my opinion, the fetus is not only contained by the mother's belly, not only a proof of the superiority of the father and of his attributes, as compared to the child and his small, infertile penis, it represents life itself, that is to say, that which, by definition, involves development and evolution. It implies, consequently, a waiting, and therefore the reality principle, which is also the case with thought.

Life, the fetus, thought, the reality principle and genitality have the same relation to each other as do death, the corpse, absence of thought, anality and the pleasure principle. We know, furthermore, that Freud, when he introduces the last topographical theory ("Beyond the Pleasure Principle," 1920), considers the pleasure principle as being in the service of the death instinct.

The patient, moreover, has motives, linked to his personal history, for bringing into the picture themes, activated by the transference, which are connected in a very obvious manner with concentration camps and Nazi crimes: babies' skulls shattered (the nuts), cremation ovens (vessels for making fondue or where meat is grilled), gas chambers, etc.

To homogenize obstacles, to render them undifferentiated, is to make them disappear as obstacles, and is to find again a way into the mother's belly.

Generally speaking, we all have, in differing degrees, and more so when we are in a group situation than when we are acting as individuals, a propensity to think in a way that "yields in the direction of least resistance" to quote Bernard Shaw, to whom Freud refers in "The Two Principles of Mental Functioning" when he wishes to demonstrate the superiority of the ego-reality over the pleasure reality. Our waking thought, when it functions according to the laws of the pleasure principle and the primary processes, ends in a complete confusion of values.

If differences are abolished, so are cause and effect. To take up again an idea of Béla Grunberger, the cause is to the effect as the father is to the child. If the paternal principle has disappeared from the world, both a before and an after, and history itself, have at the same time disappeared. Any judgment of a situation that does not take into account either the why or the how, which detaches an event from its context without putting it into perspective, participates in the thought regression that I describe here. It is a kind of thinking that is linear and nonhistorical. From a position outside the causal dimension, ideas and words can be used in any way whatsoever: it is in the name of "liberty of thought" that Noam Chomsky wrote the preface to Robert Faurisson's book, which denied the existence of gas chambers and of the Holocaust. In France, for some years, the word *amalgam* has been given to the kind of thinking that establishes relations between facts or events by taking up its position outside the causal dimension and by effacing differences of quality or quantity. For example, the Vietnam war is put on the same level as Auschwitz, or the siege of the Palestinians in Beirut is compared to events in the Warsaw ghetto during the World War II. Nazi propaganda furnished perfect examples of these amalgams when it stigmatized "the Anglo-Judeo-Bolshevik plutocracy," a series of contradictory ideas which, in German, form a single word. In the language register, where the obstacle, the father, or the cause has disappeared, or thought flows according to the line of least resistance, slogans can take the place of serious thinking, however absurd they are, like those in

George Orwell's novel *1984*: "Liberty is slavery, war is peace." The words of Vocabulary B of Newspeak clearly come under the sign of an amalgam: "B words form a sort of verbal shorthand which piles up in several syllables a series of complete ideas. The B words were not created according to an etymological plan. The words which compose them could be put anywhere one chooses."

If we all have a propensity to immerse ourselves in the easy flow of a regressive manner of thought, if the archaic matrix of the Oedipus complex is universal, as the Oedipus complex itself is universal, what then is the link between the primitive core of the Oedipus complex and perversion?

THE ARCHAIC MATRIX OF THE OEDIPUS COMPLEX AND PERVERSION

The two male patients, Alexander and Romain, both show, in differing degrees, it is true, elements of perverse behavior. Alexander experienced, during his military service, an episode of homosexual prostitution. Then he set up house with a doctor who urged him to study medicine. Today he is married, the father of a family, and has a comfortable social position. His homosexuality shows itself at first sight (on a conscious level) as an active desire for revenge against the father (the wish to take possession of him).

On the unconscious level, it is a question of being passively penetrated himself in order to fill, by acting out, the vacuum which resulted from an absence of introjection of the paternal penis: the very sensual exchanges between him and his mother, this complicity, leading to the exclusion of the father who was alcoholic and violent. The father (together with his attributes) was, at one and the same time, feared and disparaged.

Romain's sexual behavior is more complex and his perversion is more concealed. He is sexually attracted, in a conscious way, by certain men, for example by X who figures in the dream of the smooth fish. During his analysis, he wet his bed whenever he had a homosexual dream or invited a friend to spend the night with him (he is separated from his wife, who left him because he hit her). He has masturbatory fantasies that are passive and masochistic and during which he is the plaything of one or more women. He shows an important moral masochism in the sense in which Freud uses this expression in the "Economic Problem of Masochism" (1924): a resexualisation of the relations between the Ego and the Superego, which, in my opinion, should be distinguished from the self-punishment of the neurotic. The link of this moral masochism with erogenous masochism is obvious. One day Romain let himself be cheated out of money in a three-card game at a flea market. Later, after a session, he saw some men fighting. There was blood. He wanted to stop his car to separate them, but he told himself it would be stupid and dangerous. A policeman then arrived. He thought of the day when he let himself "be had" in the three-card game. He nearly went back to the same place to see if he could find those men. To be delivered, just like that, to men . . . He is carried away in thought . . . (here one can see his masturbatory fantasy reappear, but the objects now are masculine). He thinks of sex-shops . . .

He thinks also, from time to time, during a session, of Jesus on the cross. Of the lance which they thrust into his side . . . They got a lot out of him. One day his identification with Jesus Christ became consciously linked with the transference. He imagined his heart resting on a dish. Thus he offered himself to me, he said. For quite a long time, he provoked incidents with the government authorities: customs men, policemen, etc . . .

Romain, in spite of his age (he is nearly forty), steals from book-shops, which arouses him sexually to the point of erection, a process which, it seems to me, cannot be merely attributed to the eroticization of fear. In fact, these actions, are linked to his curiosity about the activities of his father during World War II. This curiosity refers, in the last analysis, to the primal scene, which is reduced to a relation between victim and executioner in a concentration camp. (The day he went into analysis, Romain learned that his father had been an Iron Guard, the Romanian equivalent of the SS, and that he had written a thesis on racial characteristics, measuring the skulls of deportees. Romain received this information as if he had always known about it, as he had known about the sexual life of his parents.) At the same time, to steal books is to take possession of the paternal penis, which he has never really introjected, among other reasons because of its dangerous quality. In the case of Romain, as in that of Alexander (and in all cases of perversion, but this is particularly obvious in homosexuality), there is something important lacking in the constitution of the Ego, because of a faulty identification with the father. The absence of a stable introjection of his penis leads to the absence of an integrated identity, to the establishment of a fragile barrier against incest, of which the father's penis is the representative, and, consequently, to important distortions in the moral agency.

Indeed, the existence of sexual deviations is not enough to define a perverse organization, and the difference in diagnosis from that of a borderline organization, at least in the case of Romain, could be questioned. I am thinking particularly of those borderline patients showing perverse polymorphous tendencies of whom O. Kernberg in *Borderline Conditions and Pathological Narcissism* (1975) writes. I would be inclined, however, to think that the presence of perverse tendencies betrays, even in borderline patients, an attempt to become anchored in the type of regression I am about to define.

I have examined elsewhere ("Reflections on the Connections between Sadism and Perversion," 1978; "Perversion and the Universal Law," 1983) the erasure the pervert tends to accomplish of the twofold difference between the sexes and the generations. In fact, he seeks the abolition of all the differences which make up reality, as I have stated earlier. It seems obvious to me, in the material of the patients discussed here, that this return to an undifferentiated state and to the state of chaos preceding the introduction of separation, of division, of distinctions, of naming, of paternal law (or, in the Bible, of the law of God) would be specific to the anal-sadistic stage to which the pervert regresses.

Romain and Alexander situate their dreams, the former in a gas chamber (where manipulation is being carried out), and the latter in a dissecting room (where corpses—excrements—are being cut up and bones extricated).

In Romain's dreams, the fondue vessels also represent his own anus, which has the ability to transform separate objects into an undifferentiated mass: a process similar to that of digestion, which also involves burning, and which reduces the most disparate elements of food to identical and homogeneous fecal particles.

In "The Two Principles of Mental Functioning," Freud states that the sexual instincts are less submissive to the reality principle than the Ego instincts. He writes: "The sexual instincts behave auto-erotically at first; they obtain their satisfaction in the subject's own body and therefore do not find themselves in the situation of frustration which was what necessitated the institution of the reality principle and when later on, the process of finding an object begins, it is soon interrupted by the long period of latency, which delays sexual development until puberty."

I have described elsewhere how the anal-sadistic phase represents a kind of sketch and a parody of genitality, referring to Freud's "On Transformation of Instincts as Exemplified in Anal Eroticism" (1917). The anal phase bestows on the child elements that enable him to claim to equal the father and his attributes, by this means leapfrogging the normal development leading to genitality. The fecal stick foreshadows the genital penis, the daily separation from the stools is the precursor of phallic castration, the production of feces anticipates the bringing of children into the world, the excrement in the rectum imitates genital coitus. When the elements of the anal phase are so taken as equivalent to genitality—as if Freud's equation: "feces = penis = child" were understood not in a metaphorical sense but as if it were real, as in Hanna Segal's symbolic equation (1957)—we find ourselves functioning according to the pleasure principle.

The child, in fact, maintains the illusion of not having to postpone the expected satisfaction. The postulated equivalence between anality and genitality aims to circumvent evolution, as if it were to conjure it away, to compress time, to make the child with his prepubertal penis equal to the father, whose genital penis and specific powers are disqualified. At the same time the child, generally upheld by the attitude of the mother, is—at least he is anxious to think so—an adequate sexual partner for her. Thus he is enabled to omit the process of identification with his father, a process whose core is the introjection of the penis.

It is true that, in order for the anal-sadistic regression to be ego-syntonic in perversion, it must be accompanied, as I have stressed elsewhere, by an *idealization* of the objects, erotogenic zones and instincts of the anal phase. It is precisely this idealization that permits the anal elements to pass through the barrier of repression. It is also this idealization that differentiates between regression in perversion and psychotic regression, because if it conceals anality it is an indication that the Ego in its totality does not ignore the anal character of its objects and instincts.[9]

So, in perversion, the subject succeeds, by means of the anal-sadistic regression and the idealization which is linked to it—and it is this which essentially distinguishes him from the psychotic—in reaching a state, within the framework of this regression, that is reached by the mental apparatus of the psychotic only by means of a narcissistic regression. We must here note that if the *denial* in the pervert applies to the genital order (to its value and its very signification), the anal-sadistic regression which comes to take its place is not equivalent to the autocratic creation of a new world by the psychotic, as described by Freud in "Neurosis and Psychosis" (1924), for the anal universe preceding that of the father exists in each one of us: we have all experienced the anal phase. The "new world" of the pervert, although it is "constructed in accordance with the desires of the Id" rests, therefore, upon a kind of reality, that of a phase of development of which we still retain vestiges.

The gap existing between the genital universe and the anal universe is, in fact, filled not with delusion but with idealization. The function of idealization is, as it is for delusion, to reconstruct bonds with reality (as Freud points out in "Neurosis and Psychosis"). I have stressed the pervert's compulsion to idealize, which explains his aesthetic affinities and which now seems to me to be the essential mechanism preventing a descent into psychosis. Romain and Alexander are both musicians, and each plays an instrument. Both have, at some time in their lives, dreamed of an artistic career.

Anal regression in perversion allows the reestablishment of the pleasure principle represented by the fantasy of making the mother's belly smooth and the destruction of the representatives of the father and of reality—without bringing about a dissolution of the Ego and its agencies.

Moreover, the pervert does not experience the horror of incest. Not only is the prohibition less absolute, because of the defective introjection of the paternal penis, the core of the Superego, but also this introjection is necessary for the establishment of sexual identity which is thus missing in the pervert. The Oedipal prohibition in the neurotic is accompanied by a sense of horror—a sacred prohibition, as Freud calls it in *Moses and Monotheism* (1939)—a horror of returning to the place from where he came, the mother's belly, for fear of losing his hard won identity. This fear is absent from those whose sexual identity has never been established (it is at its height in those nonperverts in whom the sexual identity is the most fragile). The fantasy of returning to the mother's body after having destroyed the obstacles which prevent access to it is thus easier to discern in the pervert who does not experience the sacred horror of a return to the sameness from which he originated.

It is necessary, finally, to emphasize that the archaic matrix of the Oedipus complex, if it is to be found in the evolved Oedipus complex and in the myth of Oedipus itself, is at the same time opposed to it.

Concerning the myth, Van der Sterren (*Oedipus,* 1948) interprets the murder of Laius at the junction of three roads as the murder of a father who barred access to the maternal genitals. The "Oedipal" subject does not seek to put on one side the paternal genital dimension but to take possession of it by means of identification. This implies a projection of his narcissism on the father, his penis and genitality. This process is accompanied by a capacity to wait for satisfaction, to postpone and to accept, when all is said and done, objects which are substitutes and satisfactions which are symbolic.

The destruction of reality and the access, at last recovered, to the smooth body of the mother is probably, in the last analysis, what motivates the modern cosmic imitators of Erostrates. This fantasy is at the heart of beliefs and ideologies which promise a marvelous regeneration that will spring from a terrible upheaval, as it is written in the Apocalypse: "And I saw a new heaven and a new earth: for the first earth passed away; and there was no more sea. And I, John, saw the holy City, the new Jerusalem, coming down from God out of heaven, prepared as a bride adorned for her husband . . . and there shall be no more death, neither sorrow, nor crying, neither shall there be any more pain, for the former things are passed away."

6.

THE ARCHAIC MATRIX OF THE OEDIPUS COMPLEX IN UTOPIA

Throughout the ages, writers and philosophers have described ideal cities and isles of blessedness in stories which expressed an ancient dream of a happiness which is, supposedly, common to all humanity. In the penultimate chapter of his book *History of Utopia* (1967), the sociologist Jean Servier writes: "Utopia opens out a new field of sociological thought because it is a unique way of thinking whose modes of expression have scarcely altered over the centuries . . . . All the different utopias seem, on reading them, to be like the fairy tales of a single country, to be variations on a single mythical theme: from one century to another the similarities between the work of different authors have been so great that it would seem that a common thread mysteriously unites them."[1] In other words, differences in the political, economic and social scenes in which they appeared—and their appearance is clearly linked to specific moments in history—does not undermine the persistence of certain themes. It seems to me that the psychoanalyst, as well as the sociologist, has something to say about this. He has to discover the primary fantasy which is expressed again and again unchanged in these manifestations of the human spirit. It seems to me to be possible to extract from these utopias the archaic matrix of the Oedipus complex.

According to my hypothesis there is a primary wish to rediscover a universe without obstacles, a smooth maternal belly, stripped of its contents, to which free access is desired. These contents are made up of the father, his penis, babies and excrement. Properly speaking, there is no question of a stage of the Oedipus complex, but of the representation of a mode of mental functioning without hindrances, ruled by the pleasure principle.

To find elements of this fantasy in utopias, I intend to group the various utopian themes under three headings. The first is the topography of utopia; it concerns the closed world of the island or town surrounded by its ramparts. The second examines the theme of transparency in the utopian city, which explains its social, political and economic organization by means of its architecture. The last will be that of the tabula rasa, the blank sheet, a theme which is often concealed but is nevertheless latent in a number of descriptions, and which will be accompanied by a tentative explanation of the link existing between utopias and violence and destruction, each time utopias come to be realized. I here part company with Jean Servier, who draws a line firmly between millennarianism in its different forms as they are described by N. Cohn in *The Pursuit of the Millennium* (1957) and the utopias which would result from a search for nonviolent solutions to conflicts. I define the word utopia as a description of political systems suggested as models and constructed under the aegis of rationality.[2]

THE ISLAND AND THE ENCLOSED CITY OF A UTOPIA

It has often been remarked that a utopia is situated on an island or in a city surrounded by concentric walls. These utopian islands have existed since the earliest times, in Hesiod, Homer and Pindar. Diodoros of Sicily described the "Islands of the Sun" where perfect happiness reigned. Plutarch sang of the "Fortunate Isles" and the island of Ogygia. As for the concentric walls, they are found in Atlantis (which, moreover, is an island), and described by Plato in the *Critias* as well as in Campanella's *City of the Sun* (1602), which is also on an island.

The island and the enclosed town therefore form a representation to which historical factors have given a form and a substance but which are nonetheless linked to the unconscious fantasy, which is non-historical and which we seek to uncover.

In order to understand what the closed world of the island signifies, we will start with the touching example of the story *Paul and Virginie* by Bernardin de Saint-Pierre (1788), which takes place on the Ile-de-

France (now Mauritius). At the beginning of the story, we find two women, Madame de La Tour and Marguerite, who have both given birth to fatherless children. Marguerite, abandoned by her lover, gives birth to Paul. Madame de La Tour is pregnant with Virginie when her husband dies.

At a certain moment in the story, Paul and Virginie are alone together and are hungry. "'What shall we do,' asks Paul, 'these trees give only fruit you can't eat.' 'God will take pity on us,' replied Virginie, 'He answers the prayer of little birds when they ask him for food.' Scarcely had she uttered these words, when they heard the sound of a spring which was falling from a rock nearby." We are in the realm of the pleasure principle, where wishes are immediately fulfilled. All through the story, we find a recurring subject—wishes for food are granted. Bernardin de Saint-Pierre makes it clear to us that this oral abundance is linked to the presence of a mother's breast which is always offered and never dries up. The spring comes from a mountain: "This mountain was called the Three-Breasts," because its three peaks have that shape. Here Bernardin puts in a note: "There are many mountains whose summits are rounded like breasts, and which have that name in all languages. They are indeed breasts because from them flow many of the rivers and the streams which spread abundance over the earth. . . . We have mentioned this admirable foresight on the part of nature in our earlier works." Abundance and immediate oral satisfactions occur frequently in utopias. In a similar way Rousseau quotes in *Emile* a description of the royal garden in Homer's *Odyssey* where "The inexhaustible vine never ceases to bear grapes" (Livre V). This profusion and acceleration of harvest exist also in the New Jerusalem, where the Trees of Life give fruit twelve times a year.

The island where the utopia of *Paul and Virginie* is situated and also the whole of nature, are gardens full of fruit which is always ready for taking. Thus the island possesses obvious maternal characteristics which one can also find in other literature of the period, for example in *The Shipwreck on the Floating Islands or Basiliade* of Morelly (1753): "The individual ownership which is pitiless and which engenders all the crimes flooding the rest of the world was unknown to the population. They thought of the earth as a wet-nurse for everybody, who offered her breast to her children when they felt hunger; they all felt obliged to make her fertile; but nobody said: this is my field, my ox, my dwelling." Seneca, describing the Golden Age, imagined a time when "the farmers did not till the earth, boundary-stones between fields were unknown to men, all was held in common and the earth gave freely and in abundance. All men took benefit from nature: this mother, ever watchful, gave to her children everything for their needs." The maternal breast must belong to everybody. Almost all utopias are founded on goods held in common. It is true of Plato's Republic, of More's Utopia and also of Bernardin's island, which forms an utopian society in miniature. The two mothers live in neighboring huts : "They had but one will, one interest, one table. They held everything in common." And also: "My friend, Madame de La Tour would say, we shall have two children and each of our children will have two mothers." The mothers shared their milk between the children, offering their breast to one or to the other. Here we have the idea of children being held in common, which occurs equally often in other utopias, from Plato to Fourier. In *The Republic*, it is stressed that fathers will not know their sons, nor the sons their fathers. With Thomas More, we find ourselves more often in the town than in the country. However, agriculture, as in the majority of utopias, has a special status: "Well there is an activity they all do, irrespective of sex, and that is farming; and no one can be exempted from it." Thomas More, in *Utopia,* introduces the idea of alternation of labor: "Each year twenty people from each house go back to town, having done two years in the country, and are replaced by twenty others." We can see that farming, considered as a pure and natural occupation, is not only exclusive to eighteenth-century writers, it is at the very heart of a utopia.

We find this sanctification of farming again in the industrialized society of the nineteenth century. "The earth still has all the power of a symbol in the landscape of the city of New Lanark reformed by Owen. The workers are purified by soul-enhancing work in the fields after a time spent in the factories, necessary for the good of society." Let us note also the privileged part played by agriculture and those who work on the land in the alleged utopias which have come into existence in the twentieth century, in Mao Zedong's China, in Communist Vietnam which practises the alternation of work and where inhabitants of the town, whether shopkeepers or university professors, are obliged to do "voluntary" work in the fields every year, and the Kampuchea of Pol Pot.[3] We shall return to this last example.

It is therefore a question of establishing a symbiosis with Mother Nature, who offers her children her overflowing breast to the exclusion of the father. In fact, he is absent from utopias, and the holding of children in common and the absence of inheritance which is also often mentioned lead to an effacing of the paternal image. The island and the enclosed gardens within it constitute a representation of the maternal womb in which the child finds an immediate satisfaction of his needs. So a return to the uterus and a new fusion with the mother are experienced. The inhabitants of the enchanted islands are therefore a horde of brothers who have taken possession of the mother, having banished the father.

The inhabitant of a town is he who cannot reach a symbiosis with the mother because he is far removed from nature. The town is fundamentally the enemy of the utopian world. It is because Virginie left her island of happiness to go to the town in Europe that misfortune fell on her and her family: "It is in Europe that working with your hands is dishonorable. They call it mechanical work. The most despised of all is he who tills the soil. An artisan (that is, a town-dweller) is more highly esteemed than a peasant." Paul: "What! The activity which gives men food is despised in Europe! I do not understand." The Town is an artificial creation of man, and so goes against Nature: "God makes all things good; man meddles with them and they become evil." It is with this sentence that Rousseau begins *Emile*. He also says: "Men are not made to be piled up in heaps like ants, but to be spread over the earth to cultivate it. . . . Towns are the nadir of the human spirit." Finally he writes this ecological valediction: "Farewell then to you, O Paris, famous town, town of noise, of smoke and of mud, where women think no more of honor, nor men of virtue. Farewell Paris; we seek love, happiness, innocence; we can never be far enough away from you." If this hatred of the town seems linked only to actual historical events (the beginning of the Industrial Revolution), remember that Müntzer, one of the leaders of a particularly bloody millennarist movement which was rife around 1520, advocated not only the possession of goods in common but a return to Nature, and, under the influence of a humanist, Ulrich Hugwald, held that it was the life of a peasant which came closest to God's intention. As for the dramatic events in Kampuchea, we know that the people of Phnom Penh suffered genocide precisely because they were townsfolk, while the peasants were considered to be the "bedrock of society" (see Pin Yathay: *A Murderous Utopia*).

However, towns are also found in utopias, the New Jerusalem being the supreme example. We know the town is very often shut in by walls, which we can consider as the equivalent of the natural isolation of an island, surrounded by the sea and also as representing the secret, closed universe of the womb. But the town is built to a geometric architectural plan, symmetrical and uniform.

Here is the Biblical description of the New Jerusalem: it had "a wall, great and high and had twelve gates, and at the gates twelve Angels, and names written thereon, which are the names of the twelve tribes of Israel. On the east, three gates, on the north three gates, at the west three gates, at the south three gates. And the wall of the City had twelve foundations . . . And he that talked with me had a golden reed to measure the City, and the gates thereof and the wall thereof. And the City lieth four-square, and the length is as long as the breadth: and he measured the City with the reed twelve thousand furlongs. The length and the breadth and the height of it are equal. And he measured the wall thereof, one hundred cubits . . . and the street of the City was pure gold as it were transparent glass."

Plato's city in *The Laws,* like the ideal city in *The Politics* of Aristotle, is planned on strict geometrical lines. Here is Thomas More's description of Amaurotum, the capital of Utopia: "Well, when you've seen one of them, you've seen them all, for they're nearly identical. . . . Amaurotum is built on a gently sloping hill-side, and its ground-plan is practically square. . . . The town is surrounded by a thick, high wall, with towers and blockhouses at frequent intervals. On three sides of it there's also a moat, which contains no water, but is very broad and deep, and obstructed by a thorn-bush entanglement. On the fourth side the river serves as a moat. The streets are well designed. The buildings face one another and run the whole length of the street. "Each house has a front-door leading into the street, and a back-door into the garden. In both cases they're double swing-doors, which open at a touch, and close automatically behind you. So anyone can go in and out, for there's no such thing as private property. The houses themselves are allocated by lot, and changed round every ten years."

Fourier constructs his phalanstery from a plan which, to Victor Considérant, would resemble the Palais-Royal in Paris in its symmetry. In his *Theory of Universal Unity,* Fourier reproaches the architects for having been unable to devise a *plan* for a town.

So, if island and town resemble each other in their enclosure, they appear to differ fundamentally in other ways. The town, a creation of man, and therefore artificial, far from attempting to resemble Nature more closely by being spontaneous and free, is not a construction that gives full reign to liberty, flexibility and imagination. In fact, it is as far removed from Nature as possible. Its architecture follows a strict plan. *Uniformity* and *rationality* prevail.

This uniformity and rationality can be found at all levels. Thus in several utopias the citizens wear uniforms. It is so with the dwellers in More's Utopia. The standardization of architecture spreads to all aspects of life: "There are fifty-four splendid big towns on the island, all with the same language, laws, customs and institutions. They are all built on the same plan, and, so far as the sites will allow, they all look exactly alike." There is strict regimentation: where the Utopians sit at table, the age when girls and boys marry, the number of families in the city. "Each town consists of six thousand households, not counting the country ones, and to keep the population fairly steady there's a law that no household shall contain less than ten or more than sixteen adults. . . . This law is observed by simply moving supernumerary adults to smaller households. If the town as a whole gets too full, the surplus population is transferred to a town that's comparatively empty." The town may oblige a citizen to change his occupation if it is for the common good. The Utopian day is divided into hourly sections. At the communal meal, there is one hour's recreation. This detailed planning of both the town and life in the town is typical of most utopias. It is apparently opposed to the grace and sweetness of a life lived close to nature, very evident in *Paul and Virginie:* "Paul and Virginie had neither clocks, almanacks, nor books of philosophy, history or chronology. Their life was regulated according to the rhythm of nature. They told the time by the tree's shadows and the seasons according to when they gave flowers and fruit, and the passage of time by the number of harvests. These delightful images gave the greatest charm to their conversation. 'It's dinner-time, Virginie would say to her family, the banana-trees have their shadows at their feet.'"

How can we explain this apparent contradiction between the world of the town and that of nature, if we maintain that the enclosure represents for each of them the maternal womb?

Y. Zamiatine's book, *We,* which is actually an anti-utopia, was written in Russia in 1920 but never published in that country. It can help us to resolve the difficulty.

THE THEME OF TRANSPARENCY

The Town, in Zamiatine's account, is surrounded by a Green Wall. It is built entirely of glass: "Our modern glass—splendid, transparent, eternal—" All public buildings, houses, flats, furniture and pavements are made of glass: ". . . diffused bluish light, the glass of the walls glimmering, the sight of the glass chairs, the glass table," ". . . below, the blue cupolas, the cubes of glass ice were turning a leaden hue," "The stairs leading down into the subway—and underfoot, on the immaculate glass of the steps . . . ," "I am practically the only one in the building. Through the sun-shot walls I can see far to the right and left and downward—I can see the empty rooms, suspended in the air and repeating one another like reflections in mirrors," "From the head of my bed came the brisk, crystal-clear ringing of a small bell: 7:00, time to get up. To the right and left, through the walls of glass, I seem to be seeing myself, my room, my clothes, my movements—but repeated thousands of times over. This is invigorating: one sees oneself as one enormous, mighty whole. And such precise beauty: not one superfluous gesture, deviation, turn;" "You know, I was walking on the Prospect just now, and there was a man ahead of me, and he was casting a shadow on the pavement. And you understand, his shadow was luminous! And it seems to me—no, I feel certain of it—that on the morrow there will be no shadows whatsoever—neither of a single human being nor of a single thing; everything will be shot through with sunlight."

It is obvious that this universe is one of *transparency*. It symbolizes that the citizens of the town are completely revealed to each other, all dividing walls having disappeared. They reflect each other as the houses and rooms are reflected. There must be a single identity among the citizens, who, in addition, are identified by numbers. Privacy no longer exists, as is symbolized by the perfect transparency of the walls. It is only during their "Sexual Days," which are determined by a table, calculated by the laboratories of the Sexual Bureau, that members have the right to use curtains. Everything that in any way distinguishes one citizen from another has gone: "Ordinarily, however, we constantly live in full sight of all, constantly bathed in light and surrounded by our glass walls that seem to be woven of coruscating air. . . . Quite possibly it may have been the opaque habitations of the ancients which engendered their pitiful cellular psychology." To put it in other words, the regimentation of life—for the members wear uniforms—is due to the need to reduce the citizens to a single entity, a single body. This is something that Zamiatine expresses very well when he makes his hero chant the praises of the Table of Commandments: "The Tables of Hourly Commandments, however, really does transform each one of us into the six-wheeled steel hero of a great poem. Each morning, with six-wheeled precision, at the very same minute and the very same second we, in our millions, arise as one. At the very same hour we mono-millionedly begin work—and when we finish it, we do so mono-millionedly. And, *merging into but one body* [emphasis added] with multimillioned hands, at the very second designated by the Tables of Hourly Commandments we bring our spoons up to our mouths." And later also: "We were walking the way we usually do—i.e., as the marching warriors are depicted on Assyrian monuments: a thousand heads, two composite integrated legs, two integrated swinging arms." The will of the individual no longer exists. All private interests fuse into the general will, according to the social consensus, for the sake of Common Good, to mention some of the expressions dear to writers of utopias.

It is obvious that here we have an excellent description of totalitarianism; this is what Zamiatine wishes the reader to understand. I believe that there is continuity between this universe of transparency and the architecture, institutions, laws and customs of utopian systems. Zamiatine has, in fact, made clear and open to interpretation a feature of utopian cities which is difficult to comprehend, even, one supposes, by their inventors. I mean their geometrical quality, their symmetry, their uniformity.

If there exists, as I believe from my clinical experience, a fantasy of reintegrating the mother's smooth belly, emptied of its contents, it follows that the complete realization of this fantasy applied to nature would end in an eradication of the human species to the benefit of the single Self. Utopias in general and utopian towns in particular seem to me to be attempts to reconcile wishes linked to the existence of the archaic matrix of the Oedipus complex with the exigencies of life in a society. Since nobody can keep for himself alone either the earth mother or the ideal city, one must act in such a way that the horde of brothers who have taken possession of the mother will form a single entity, a single body. As Zamiatine writes: "We walked along, a single million-headed body, and within each of us was the meek joyfulness which, probably, constitutes the life of molecules, atoms and phagocytes. In the world of antiquity this was understood by the Christians, our only (even though very far from perfect) predecessors: meekness is a virtue, while pride is a vice; they also understood that We is from God, while I is from the Devil."

It can here be noted that, in fact, Christianity goes still further in reducing all Christians to a single body. Paul says in the Epistle to the Romans that, "just as our body in its unity possesses more than one member, and these members do not have all the same function, so we, though many, are but one body in Christ, being members one of another." He exhorts, in the Epistle to the Philippians: "Be one mind, one accord, one sentiment." In the Epistle to the Colossians, he writes to the Christians who are assembled in "one body." The Christian aspiration, in the last analysis, is to reduce humanity to a single being, to a single mystical body. As for the idea of the one flock, it existed before Christian times. Plutarch, in *On the Fortune of Alexander,* reports that Zeno of Citium was supposed to have described a republic where "all men are fellow citizens, for whom there is but one life, one order of things, as for a flock united under the rule of one shepherd."

There is a basic *passion for unity* in utopia (to use one of Fourier's expressions). Thanks to the perfect union of bodies and minds ("That is true even of thoughts, you understand. That is because nobody is *one*, but *one of*. We are so alike" [p. 24]), each minute part of this gigantic organism with its millions of cells can feel an identity with the whole organism: "I saw the irrevocable straight streets, the ray-spurting glass of the roadways, the divine parallelepipedons of the transparent dwellings, the square harmony of our grey-blue ranks. And so it struck me that it had not been the generations upon generations but I—precisely I—who had conquered the old God and the old life: that is precisely I who had created all this. And, as if I were a tower, I was afraid to move my elbow lest I send the walls, cupolas, machines tumbling in a cascade of fragments." It is only possible to attain this affect of elation and megalomania if there is in the city a perfect consensus, an ideal harmony, an absolute "monophonie." The least obstacle, dare I say the least dissent, threatens the entire system by making it impossible for each "number" to achieve this megalomaniac identification of his Self with the whole mass. So it is that the smallest grain of sand in the wheels of the gigantic machine will be expelled mercilessly. So, the Benefactor gets rid of the criminal by reducing him to a chemically pure puddle of water (even the bodies of the citizens have lost their opacity).

Thus it seems that what appears to some as a horrible totalitarian society is, for others—advocates of utopias, have inevitably a totalitarian character, though this is often unconscious—the fulfilment of the wish to return to the mother's womb, supported by the achievement of a perfect unity in the body of society. "The totalitarian temptation," the title of a book by J.F. Revel, cannot be understood, to my mind, by a simple reference to sadomasochism but by the seductive powers of fantasies linked to the archaic matrix of the Oedipus complex. The perfectly straight streets, the rigorous geometry of the buildings, the sameness of the houses, the passion for numbers which exists in most utopias, together form a whole, apparently antagonistic to nature and purely rationalistic, which aims to break divisions between minds, and to create a single being which will take possession of the mother. The father is, by definition, excluded from this universe of identical particles, since differences no longer exist, and the classification into fathers and sons implies the persistence of differences.

We know that, for Freud, in the human being there is a tendency of the psychic apparatus to maintain at as low a level as possible the quantity of excitations. It is the principle of constancy. When Freud expresses the idea that the psychic apparatus tends to reduce excitations to zero, he introduces the principle of Nirvana linked to the death-instinct. These two principles are closely connected to the pleasure principle which, seen in an economic perspective, would be linked to the avoidance of tensions. A universe without differences is a universe without tensions. It is this that Zamiatine perceives very clearly: ". . . I must remark at this point that the process of the induration, the crystallization of life is, apparently, still incomplete, even among us. There are still a few steps left to attain the ideal. The ideal (it is clear) exists when nothing any longer happens." Here we find an echo of the speech of Enjolras on the barricades in *Les Misérables* by Victor Hugo. Having predicted that "the twentieth century will be happy" as the result of the French Revolution and of the Terror of 1793, he lists all the benefits that the twentieth century will bring with it, and exclaims: "We could almost declare that there will be no more events. We'll be happy . . ." "As for Happiness . . ." says Zamiatine's hero. "Well, now, desires are excruciating things, after all—isn't that so? And it is clear that happiness comes into existence only when there are no longer any desires—not even a single one."

Influenced by a woman who bears a strange X on her face (the unknown), Zamiatine's hero thinks: "Look: there are two forces in this world—entropy and energy. The first leads to beatific quietism, to a happy equilibrium, the second to excruciatingly perpetual motion." Later we read: "Isn't it clear to you that it is only in differences— differences!—in temperature, only in thermal contrasts, that life lies? But even if everywhere, throughout the universe, there are only equally warm—or equally cold—bodies, they must be thrust out of the way—so that there may be fire, explosion, Gehenne."

I consider that the universe of *We* opens utopias in general to interpretation. This can be not only on the level of undivided and identical contents which are welded into a single body but also on the level of the container, the image of the smooth belly of the mother representing a mental functioning without hindrances. My hypothesis seems to be confirmed by the splendid metaphor which describes the emotional upheaval of the hero when his mathematical certainties are shaken by his meeting with the woman with the X on her face: "The city below seemed to be made entirely of blue ice. Suddenly a cloud cast a fleeting oblique shadow; the ice below turned to a leaden hue; it swelled up. That's the way it happens in spring, when you are standing on the river bank, expecting everything to start cracking, surging, swirling, rushing at any moment; minute after minute passes, however, yet the ice remains stationary, and you yourself feel that you are swelling, your heart pounds still more restlessly, still more frequently—however, why am I writing about this since, after all, there is no ice-breaker that could possibly break the most translucent, the most solid crystal of our life."

At the beginning of the book, the hero cannot bear anything to disturb the smooth nature of the universe surrounding him; for instance, clouds in a sky which ought to be "sterile, irreproachable," a tear upon a sheet of paper. "That was still the same 'softening of the surface,' whereas the surface must be hard as a diamond, as hard as our walls." When he gets through the Wall with the unknown woman to reach the "savage condition of freedom," he does not find the smooth, pure, hard glass to which he is used in the town: "The sun—it was no longer that sun of ours, proportionately distributed over the mirror-like surface of the pavements; this sun consisted of some sort of living splinters of incessantly bobbing spots which blinded one's eyes, made one's head go round . . . ; the surface underfoot was not a flat plane— not a flat plane, you understand, but something repulsively soft, yielding, alive, green, springy."

The mother's belly is no longer smooth and accessible only to the townsfolk who are fused into a unity; it is swarming with uncontrollable life. The numbers are deprived of hair. They too are pure and smooth, which contributes to their transparency and, at the same time, confers upon them the characteristics of the maternal belly. I have been able to observe, in clinical material, the wish to make the genitals of the parents smooth by depriving them of hair, as a sign of their sterility. Compare Zamiatine: "The Auditorium: an enormous half-globe of glass massifs shot through with sunlight. Circular rows of noble, globular, closely clipped heads."

Zamiatine's hero is ashamed of his hairy hands, the result of a "ridiculous atavism." On the other side of the wall men are hairy. If an "ideal *nonfreedom*" is a characteristic of the town and if a life ordered according to absolute rules and based on the divine laws of arithmetic frees man from doubt, anxiety, uncertainty and distress, and ensures for him a sense of perfect security, the problem seems to me to go beyond the old debate about the opposition between security and liberty. Liberty, in fact, is linked to the existence of differences and so to the existence of the Father and of reality, with all the tensions it brings with it. Security is linked to the avoidance of tensions, to the immediate satisfaction of wishes before they can even declare themselves: the children are asleep in the mother's womb. So the paradox of a return to nature and its laws, to innocence and plenty, which coexist in utopias with the supremacy of mathematics, with absolute regimentation, with technology and rationality, seems to me more comprehensible if one thinks of utopias as searching to apply the fantasy of a return to the mother by taking into account the inevitable social condition of man.

We have already half-perceived, not only in Zamiatine, who, as an anti-utopist emphasizes them specially, but also in utopias proper, certain features of violence which I shall group under the heading of "tabula rasa" or "blank sheet."

TABULA RASA

It is not only millennial movements which are anti-Semitic: Norman Cohn has shown that millennnarianism is drenched in Jewish blood. There are a number of utopian writings which are more or less openly anti-Semitic. Bacon, in *New Atlantis,* would deport the Jews to a neighboring island where, if they committed blasphemy, they would be

punished with the utmost severity. Already Thomas More was de-
nouncing Judaism when he drew a contrast between Christian law,
which expresses God's fatherly kindness toward His children, and the
Mosaic law, which was harsh and revengeful, designed for slaves and
brutes. Here is a quotation from Fourier, only one among many, describing a Jewish banker to whom he gives the name Iscariot: "His
trickery never came to light, because Jews employ only other Jews and
they are a people who are the secret enemies of all mankind" (*Theory of
the Four Movements,* 1808).

The anti-Semitic rages of Proud'hon are well known. It is outside the
scope of this chapter to judge the scientific or utopian nature of Marx's
work, but his *Reply to Bruno Bauer about the Jewish Question* contains passages of anti-Semitism which are equally well known. The Jew,
who has remained faithful to the Old Testament, is the representative of
the Father. Moreover, he is the object of projections of anality. The
Father, his penis, the excrements are the contents of the maternal belly
which must be eliminated. Utopias, even when they lay claim to univer-
sality, are, in the first instance, constructed for an elite. They involve an
initial exclusion and elimination of a part of the population. Everything
that would prevent the establishment of utopian bliss must be annihilated. This is made clear in an anonymous booklet that came out two
years before the French Revolution, entitled *How to Change the World*:
"What a strange dream it is of a communist society where all citizens
are fed by the state, even the menus for lunch and dinner being drawn
up for every day of their life. . . . A thousand towns, each with a cir-
cumference of two leagues must be built in France, as well as 15,000
villages and 330,000 farms. As for the towns and villages already in
existence, they will be razed to the ground." It is clear that, for the most
part, utopias are far from being so explicit. The apocalyptic phase
which comes before the establishment of the New Jerusalem is absent
from the majority of them, except in cases when they openly claim to be
established by means of a revolution. In this respect, it is interesting to
find in Fourier a hallucinatory description of the changes in climate
which will take place in the harmonian world and which will end with
the disappearance of sea creatures—and Fourier rejoices in this. This
process "amongst other benefits, will change the taste of the sea. . . .
This breaking up of the constituents of sea water, by the boreal fluid is
one of the necessary preliminaries to the creation of new life in the sea
. . . which will take the place of the horrible legions of sea monsters

which will be annihilated by immersion in this boreal fluid. . . . This sudden extinction will purge the Ocean of these disgusting creatures. . . . They will be seen to be struck down at one fell swoop."

This phase of destruction of the contents of the mother's belly is also clearly referred to by Zamiatine: "But in the thirty-fifth year before the founding of the One State, the food we eat today, a derivation of naphtha, was devised. True, only 0.2 of the population of the terrestrial globe survived; but then, cleansed of its millennial filth, how flourishing the face of the earth became! Then, too, the surviving two tenths certainly came to know bliss in the many mansions of the One State." It is, in fact, a question of ridding the earth, the maternal belly, of its defilements, and we know that everything which is the object of negative projections can be fecalized. But it is also clear that everything that symbolizes anality or devouring is excluded from utopia, or rendered valueless. Forms of currency disappear. The Utopians turn their gold into chamberpots. Fourier writes: "To try to expose the schemes of the Stock Exchange and its members would be a labour of Hercules. I doubt this demi-god felt as much disgust when cleansing the Augean stables as we feel when we delve into this cloaca of moral filth which in the Stock Exchange is called rigging the market or brokerage" (*La Phalange,* 1848).

Most of the citizens of utopias are vegetarians. But those of More's Utopia are not: ". . . there are special places outside the town where all blood and dirt are first washed off in running water. The slaughtering of livestock and cleaning of carcasses is done by slaves. . . . It is also forbidden to bring anything dirty or unhygenic inside the town, for fear of polluting the atmosphere and so causing disease." Another translation, written in More's time, speaks of "filthiness and ordure" which are washed away.

But if the four horsemen of the Apocalypse have devastated everything in their path, making the mother's belly smooth by ridding it of the representatives of the father, and of excrements, the work of violence and destruction is by no means over.[4] We have seen that the possession of the mother's body by the brothers, in order that the fantasy of a return to the mother's womb may be accomplished and the womb made accessible, must be achieved by reducing the multitude of the brothers to a single entity. So it is that any citizen who tries to escape from this law, which is upheld by an infinite number of rules affecting every aspect of life, acts against the principle of identity, creates a difference and so becomes a representative of the father. He must, therefore, be closely watched and severely punished. The clearest proof he could give of his wish to subvert the system is to abandon it, to leave the magic circle of the island. As More writes, "If you are caught without permission outside your own district you are brought home in disgrace, and severely punished as a deserter. For a second offense the punishment is slavery." This law is also advocated by Rousseau (*Le contrat social,* 1760).

In *We* Zamiatine writes: "There, beyond the wall, were the acute black triangles of some birds or other, cawing, they threw themselves into the attack, breasting the impenetrable fence of electric waves—then, repelled, soared again the wall."

Thus the island or the wall is no longer a protection but a trap which closes on its prey; the dream turns to nightmare and the gentle maternal womb changes into a sadistic anus. For if the islands are enchanted places, they are also traps where murders are committed (for instance, *The Story of Count Zarhoff, The Ten Little Niggers, The Island of Doctor Moreau, Lord of the Flies*).

I would like, in concluding, to quote from two books written approximately at the same time. They show how the garden of delights—image of the mother's womb—can turn into a murderous anal trap: "This spot, very close to the house but can in no way be perceived, a covered walk completely hides all sight of it. The thick surrounding foliage will allow no eye to penetrate it and it is always kept carefully locked. I was hardly inside before the door was hidden by the branches of alder and hazel which left only two narrow passageways on each side. When I turned round I could no longer see where I had entered, and perceiving no door, I felt as if I had fallen from the sky." Thus Rousseau begins his description of Julie's marvellous orchard in *La Nouvelle Heloïse* (part IV, XI).

"Six circles of holly and thorn-bush, each three feet thick made it impossible to perceive this house. . . . From whichever direction one looked it could only appear to be part of the forest. . . . The vault of this building was completely covered by a very thick layer of lead in which were planted different evergreen shrubs which mingled with the surrounding hedges to produce an overwhelming impression of a real hill of greenery.

"You must by now have realized that the enclosure of the house was such that, even supposing that the bars on the windows were broken and one escaped by means of the windows, freedom would still be far away because one would still have to cross the living hedges, the seventh wall surrounding them, and the great ditch around the whole." This garden, which is at once a snare and a delusion, is described by the Marquis de Sade in *La Nouvelle Justine ou les Malheurs de la Vertu* (vol. VI).

7.
"THE GREEN THEATER":
AN ATTEMPT AT INTERPRETATION
OF GROUP MANIFESTATIONS OF
UNCONSCIOUS GUILT

I have been interested in Germany for a long time. Two years of chairing the Program Committee of the first Congress of the International Psycho-Analytical Association to take place on German soil since 1932 have led me to focus my interest not only on the past of Germany, on its history and culture, but also on its present.

I read in the *Frankfurter Allgemeine* (in an article by Rainer Appell dated August 6, 1985) that when I got up to speak to the Congress at its opening ceremony in the language that was Freud's, a curse (ban) was lifted. It is always bad for people to feel cursed, bad for them and bad for others. Of course, the feeling that one is cursed is far from being of external origin only, and a certain sternness on the part of the outside world may sometimes lessen the severity of the Superego. But the very acute guilt of an Ego faced with a gigantic task, a measureless work of reparation, is experienced as an assault on the Ego by a demanding and pitiless agency. The maleficent attacks by the Superego are then projected onto the objects, which are attacked in their turn, further increasing the guilt and anxiety. This vicious circle is well-known and the kind of guilt brought into play cannot be worked through as such, because there are no feelings of sorrow or pity,[1] just terror and persecution. Thus an external curse inevitably increases the Ego's feelings of helplessness and distress and renders the process of working through depression more difficult.

My attention has been focused on the problem of German guilt. It will come as no surprise to learn that an analyst is concerned with the problem of guilt. Where are the traces of German guilt to be found? It is frequently said that Germans practice denial with regard to their past, and particularly with regard to the extermination of the Jews. The division of time into "before Auschwitz" and "after Auschwitz" to which French intellectuals so often refer, is unknown to them. Moreover, any attempt to tackle the problem on the part of the sons and daughters of that generation that have known or played a part in Nazism is met with a wall of silence. But as psychoanalysts, we know that guilt must find an outlet in which to express itself. My hypothesis is that shreds of what the parents, or even the grandparents, have denied, reappear in the children or grandchildren, and that these are not entirely unrecognizable, distorted, disconnected and colorless though they may be. The different pieces have to be assembled, the blanks have to be filled in, the creases have to be smoothed out, some fragments have to be turned the other way round and then there will be no mistaking the immortal specters from the past.

FIRE FROM HEAVEN

Certain individual clinical cases which I am unable to use here for reasons of confidentiality, do in fact confirm this view. I shall quote a short clinical vignette which bears out this belief that whatever the parents deny reappears in disguised form in the members of the next generation, despite the fact that its protagonists are Jews and not Germans, and victims, not persecutors. I suspect that the mechanisms involved in this return of the denied are similar in both cases. The patient's father had a family in Poland composed of a wife and three children. When the Nazis invaded Poland, the wife and the three children were shut into a wooden synagogue which was set on fire. The father was hiding when this happened. He escaped, enduring many hardships throughout the war. At one point, while he was staying in the ghetto of a Polish town, he met a woman who had also succeeded in surviving the persecutions. At the end of the war they went to France, married and had a new family of three children. He never spoke of his past to the "new" children who had unknowingly replaced the dead children. When my patient was thirteen or fourteen years old, he was told his father's story by a cousin. Sometime after my patient's analysis had begun, his younger brother, who knew nothing of this story, at least on a conscious level, became psychotic. His brother was then a student and in the first manifestation of his delusion he thought the Polish maid whom his parents employed was actually the wife of Franck, the General Gauleiter of Poland during the Nazi occupation. In this case, everything the parents had denied and which the son is consequently unable to integrate, reappears in the guise of a delusion, after the well-known formula of Freud: "That which was abolished internally, returns from without." During my patient's analysis, traces of his father's story and of his first family did indeed reappear, within the transference, but not in a psychotic way. I shall not go into the details. I simply wish to stress something that we as analysts know, namely that whatever has been denied by an individual, *or by the objects with whom he is supposed to identify,* will always reappear, in an inescapable, tragic, often psychotic way, in him or in his children. And when the guilt of a nation has not been worked through, when the deeds and the misdeeds of its parents have been denied, what then?

A play by Martin Walser, *Schwarzer Schwann* (*The Black Swan*) revolves around a young man, Rudi, who has recently graduated from high school but has refused his diploma.[2] On the grounds that he is suffering from a "nervous" disorder, Rudi is taken by Goothein, his father, a neurologist himself, to consult Professor Liberé. We understand that Goothein has spent four years in jail and that Liberé, who is equally guilty, has avoided punishment by changing his name (his real name is Leibniz), wiping out the past to the point of making his daughter, Irm (Hedi, in fact) believe that they have spent their lives in India. The denied past surges up again when his wife, in speaking of their lives in India, recalls memories of Benares, the funeral pyres on the banks of the Ganges and the cremation of the corpses. Rudi accuses himself of having been the author of a letter, dated March 2, 1942, from Rosenwang:

Re Action 14 f 13 in the concentration camp, referring to disposal Leader of the Dora Administrative Group, Dora-Ida underlined, I underlined, AZ underlined, period, colon 14 f 13, 0 underlined, th, S underlined, secret underlined.

Agenda. Number 3 underlined – 4 underlined – 4 – 3. To the Kommandantur of Gross-Rosen Camp. In our opinion, March 24 1942 seems to be the appropriate date for delivery since we are going to be supplied by other concentration camps in the meantime, and for technical reasons, we need to postpone the date of delivery. If the prisoners can be delivered by omnibus, we suggest two deliveries transporting 107 prisoners each. One on Tuesday March 24 and the other on Thursday March 26. Please notify the Public Services Company for the Transportation of Patients of these dates. We trust that you will come to a final decision on this matter and keep us informed so that the necessary arrangements can be made.

Signed: Rudolf Goothein

We are given to understand that the prisoner/patients are to be delivered for the purposes of experimentation. Rudi used to point his finger at them, indicating those who were to go to the left and those who were to go right. Hedi, a young girl he ordered to the right, went to the left. She was the one to call him "Schwarzer Schwann." He tells Irm, Liberé's daughter, that linen will never be clean again, that it will always be damp, whereas when his mother was alive, it was crisp and white. His mother could not stand the soot which settled on the linen. At that time there were a lot of black men (the SS wore black uniforms). His father must have been a baker, because he had an oven. His mother's death seems to be veiled in mystery. Liberé asks Goothein to tell his son that he was the one to write the letter. Goothein refuses, on the pretexts that Rudi is too sensitive, or that they are too close and that it would ruin their beautiful relationship, etc. At the end of the play Rudi commits suicide.

I have recently reread Thomas Mann's admirable *Listen Germany,* republished in France under the title *Appels aux Allemands* (Balland/ Martin Flinker, Paris, 1985). This is a collection of messages to his fellow countrymen, broadcast each month over the BBC between 1940 and 1945, when Thomas Mann was in exile in the United States. Even if he had been the only German to resist Nazism with such lucidity, one could not seek to lay the blame on all Germans alike. It is indeed striking to see how important a role the theme of guilt plays in these short and rousing messages, guilt being what he considers the motivating force behind the perversity and the persistance in evil for fear of the supreme punishment. For example, in September of 1941, speaking to his fellow countrymen of Schiller's *History of Thirty Years' War,* he said:

"At that time men feared," wrote Schiller, *"that they would suffer cruelties at the hands of the enemy equal to those they well knew they would inflict them-*

selves in similar circumstances." Is that not an accurate description of why the German people believe that they must pursue this pointless and un-winnable war to its bitter end, that they must suffer endlessly and follow their desperate leaders ever onwards to God knows what terrible conclusion? The German people are afraid that if they leave their leaders in the lurch, they will suffer what they know full well the Nazis, if victorious, would inflict on their enemies: that is, *total destruction.* The concept of genocide and the extermination of a race is a *Nazi* idea; it does not enter into the democratic way of thinking. What must be exterminated, if we are to save mankind from the most loathsome form of slavery that has ever disfigured the face of the earth, is the Nazi regime, it is Hitler and his accomplices, and not the German people.

In November, 1941, Thomas Mann again said: "Three hundred thousand Serbs have been killed, not *in the course* of the war you waged against their country, but after it, and by you, the German people, at the behest of the infamous rabble which rules over you. The unspeakable crimes which have been perpetrated now, in Russia, and against the Poles and Jews, you know about them, but you prefer not to know out of a wholly justifiable fear that equally unspeakable crimes will be committed against you; out of fear that the hatred which is growing to colossal proportions will, one day, when the strength of your people and of your machines is exhausted, fall upon you and engulf you." Mann considers that the very desperation with which the Germans fight is to be attributed to this fear of punishment after the crime, a fear that is exploited by the Nazi leaders: "From now on, you feel you have to hold out to the very last, or you will suffer the tortures of Hell." On Christmas Eve, 1941, Thomas Mann broadcast a special message: "German people, what are your thoughts on this feast day of peace; the feast of the birth of light, when Compassion born for man descended to earth? Am I right in thinking that you are filled with shame and an overwhelming longing—a longing to be innocent, to be free of the weight of the tremendous guilt under which you writhe? [. . .] Look around you and see what you have done!"

In January 1942, Thomas Mann's message took on a desperate tone, in which one can detect great anger:

The news sounds unbelievable, but my sources are good. According to reports I have received, there is terrible grief in numerous Dutch Jewish families, in Amsterdam and other cities, where they mourn their sons who have met a horrifying death. Four hundred young Dutch Jews have been deported to Germany, to be used as guinea-pigs in experiments with poison gas. The virulence of this method of waging war, chivalrous and essentially German, a real Siegfried weapon, has proved itself against these young men, members of an inferior race. They are dead, killed for the sake of the New Order and to prove the skill of the master race in waging war. They were just about good enough for that purpose: they were Jews.

As I said, this story sounds incredible, and over the whole world, people will have difficulty in believing it. [. . .] The tendency . . . not to mention the inclination to regard such accounts as invented horror stories is widely diffused, and acts to the advantage of the enemy. But they are not mere stories—they are *history*. The longer the war lasts, the more desperately this people will be caught up in their guilt [. . .] you feel you have gone too far to be able to retreat, because you are seized with terror at the thought of liquidation, of reckoning, of expiation. [. . .] It is not *victory* that you must have, because that you cannot have. The expiation which you fight to avoid must be your own work, the work of the German people, whose armies, soon to be worn down and exhausted, form a part of it. It must come from within you . . . for only vengeance and punishment can come from outside—not *purification* [. . .] Any reform is a matter for the Germans themselves, and must be their concern alone.

In February 1942, Thomas Mann urged the German people "upon whose shoulders your Führer has laid such a weight of guilt, enough to make you cringe with horror" to get rid of the Nazis and to become "a people whom others can live with," before the cries of "The Nazis must be annihilated" turn into cries of "The Germans must be annihilated."

In April of 1942, Thomas Mann gave a special broadcast to mark the first anniversary of the destruction of Coventry by Goering's airforce, as follows:

. . . one of the most horrifying exploits by which Hitler's Germany has taught the world what total war is. It began in Spain [. . .] The memory of the massacres in Poland is also one that can never die . . . it is exactly what is called a glorious chapter of history. And Rotterdam, where in twenty minutes thirty thousand people were killed in an act of bravura which is difficult to distinguish from moral lunacy. Did Germany think that she would never have to pay for the crimes which her advance into barbarism had authorized her to commit? She has hardly begun to pay . . . in the Channel and in Russia. And also what the Royal Air Force has so far managed to bring about in Cologne, Düsseldorf, Essen, Hamburg and other cities is only a beginning [. . .] I am thinking of Coventry and I have no objection to the theory that everything must be paid for. [. . .]

Hitler's Germany has neither tradition nor a future. She knows only how
to destroy and it is destruction that she will herself suffer.

In May of 1942, Thomas Mann exclaimed: "Too much has happened,
mankind has suffered too many atrocities in their readiness to yield to
temptation and to intoxication, and in their political immaturity [. . .]
Such excesses have to be paid for, and Germany has indulged in excesses which truly cry out to heaven for vengeance."

On September 27, 1942, Thomas Mann returned to the theme of
guilt and vengeance:

> We would really like to know what you think, in your heart of hearts, of
> the behavior of those who before the world act in your name—of the
> atrocities against the Jews in Europe, for example. You continue to sup-
> port Hitler's war, and tolerate the most terrible excesses out of fear of what
> a defeat would bring, of the vengeance that the nations of Europe, per-
> secuted by you, would wreak against everything that is German. Yet, from
> the Jews in particular you need fear no such vengeance. Of all your vic-
> tims, they are the most defenceless, the most averse to violence and blood-
> shed . . . and when the worst befalls you, as it probably will—the Jews,
> impassive and made wise by age, will counsel against paying like with
> like—they will perhaps be your only friends and advocates in the world.[3]

On October 15, 1942, Thomas Mann addressed himself to the Germans living in America, refuting the propaganda of Goebbels and as-
suring them that it was no one's intention to annihilate Germany:
"What must be exterminated is the spirit of evil which is in control of
Germany at the present time."

On November 29 of the same year, he stated that a Nazi victory
would be "intolerable and indefensible" and would lead to "the annihilation of the German people and its exclusion from human society."

On May 25, 1943, Thomas Mann described the reactions in the
United States on the tenth anniversary of the auto-da-fé of May 10,
1933, that day on which the Nazis set huge bonfires of books on fire.
"The flag over the New York Public library had been lowered to half-
mast and posters, printed by the American Office of Propaganda,
showed the followers of Hitler, the destroyers of civilization, being
suffocated by the smoke coming from the burning funeral pyres of
books."

On October 30, 1943, Thomas Mann spoke of the air raids of which
Germany was then the constant target: "The bestiality of the Nazis,

their vandalism, their stupid and vicious cruelty, and the general enor-
mity of their crimes, of which you Germans can have only a faint
conception . . ." does not preclude feelings of commiseration for the
hardships endured by German civilians:

> But the way in which the Nazi press dwells upon these disasters, the way
> they exploit them as a means of exculpating themselves, so as to lay the
> blame, which by right should fall upon fascist Germany, upon their adver-
> saries, blame for the curse of barbarism and violation of rights which they
> well know they have themselves laid upon mankind; their way of acting as
> if Nazi Germany were guiltless of any crime but were herself the victim,
> subjected to the criminal fury of destructive attacks . . .

Das schwarze Korps, the official publication of the Gestapo, contains
indignant and moralizing accounts of "crimes committed against humanity" and:

> Anyone reading these clever articles without remembering and recogniz-
> ing all that Nazi Germany has inflicted upon other peoples since she began
> her devilish war of plunder and rapine; anyone ignoring the state of
> foolhardy and supercilious intoxication with their own superiority which
> the country has revelled in for years, or its pride in its triumphant crimes;
> anyone not remembering Warsaw, and Rotterdam, and London, and Cov-
> entry and the exultant descriptions of an assuaged thirst for cruelty with
> which the German press has reported these actions . . . would break out
> into a cold sweat of fear on reading them, fear for the future of the Anglo-
> Saxon powers who clearly have no other recourse than to feel suffocated
> by guilt and to sink under the weight of their heinous crimes.

Mann added: "Revenge and expiation? Here they are. And it is the
German people who are paying for its madness and its delusions [. . .]
Do you have to be told that the evils you are suffering today do not arise
from the cruelty and brutality of your enemies, but are all the result of
National Socialism?"
On May 29, 1944, Thomas Mann denounced:

> . . . the devil of German propaganda which recently vomited forth and
> denounced as barbaric murder, the inevitable cruelties of the air warfare
> which must be waged to liberate Europe [. . .] "He who sows the wind,
> reaps the whirlwind." It may well be that you Germans did not believe the
> Anglo-Saxon peoples were capable of what they are now doing. But it is
> only a reflection of what Nazi Germany has inflicted on others and still con-
> tinues to inflict upon them. You have only a terrible presentiment of this.

The theme of the evil deed and its expiation, so very apparent in Thomas Mann's monthly broadcasts, is not specific to him alone. At about the same period it can be found, for example, in the first tract distributed in Munich by the student group, "The White Rose" during the summer of 1942, where one reads the following: "Is not every honest German ashamed of his government today? Who can imagine how heavily we and our children will be burdened by the weight of this infamy, once the blindfold that deprives us of our sight today, falls, leaving us staring, open-eyed, at the absolute atrocity of these crimes?"[4] Their last tract speaks of "the shame [that] will weigh on Germany forever if its young men and women do not rise against these tormentors and crush them."

At a Mass held just after the Kristallnacht, the Catholic priest, Bernhardt Lichtenberg, asked the faithful to pray "for non-Aryan Christians and Jews. We know what happened yesterday; we do not know what will happen tomorrow, but we have seen and lived through the events of today. Look, the synagogue is in flames and the synagogue, too, is the house of God . . ." In 1941, he learned that euthanasia was being used on the mentally ill and sent a letter of protest to the authorities condemning "these unspeakable crimes." He was put into prison and then transferred to Dachau: "The weight of crimes committed against the laws of humanity lies heavily on my soul." Helmut Hesse, the son of a Protestant minister, died in Dachau in 1943, of an "injection" administered because he had protested against the persecution of the Jews and had helped Jews to hide. His father held that the recent bombing of Eberfeld might be a sign of "the justice of God." It was at this time that both men were arrested by the Gestapo and deported.

The reason I have dwelt on these texts in which the underlying theme of crime and punishment is so recurrent and where the terrible bombings that Germany suffered, especially from 1943 onward, are seen by German anti-Nazis as the beginning of the expiation, is that echoes of these themes can, in my opinion, be detected in a distorted and persecutory form in Germany today. Granted, this problem is primarily the concern of Germans, but once again, the world is involved with them.

In his book *La force du vertige*,[5] André Glücksmann speaks of the Green Movement's Nuremberg Tribunal (February 18–20, 1983). In the light of the anti-Nazi texts I have quoted above, it is extremely instructive to read the opening article of the brochure containing the

records of this trial. Written by Joachim Wernicke, it is entitled
"Purpose and Structure of the Tribunal." From the way the argumenta-
tion is developed, it becomes perfectly clear that atomic war culminat-
ing, of necessity, in the destruction of Germany, is in fact but another
example, taken to its very extreme, of a process which began with the
bombing of German towns by the Allied air forces. Moreover, the
author places the Anglo-Saxon democracies, whose bombing of civil-
ian targets is no longer seen as the consequence of Nazi crimes, in a
category with the Nazis, even holding them as more essentially evil:

> In September 1939, the British Air Force was ordered not to bomb
> civilian targets. This wise decision remained in effect until May 10, 1940.
> On that day,[6] Winston Churchill, who was in favor of air warfare, became
> Prime Minister. The same day, the German Air Force accidentally bombed
> Freiburg. Goebbels, the German Minister of Propaganda, covered up the
> incident by declaring that it was a deliberate air attack by the British Air
> Force. This is how civilian populations became the target of British and
> German warfare. At the end of 1942, the German Air Force was still not
> powerful enough to bomb England. On the other hand the British air
> fleet was formidably well organized. The United States of America en-
> tered the war, joining England in its air attacks. At first, however, the
> Americans limited their bombing to day attacks on industrial targets,
> obtaining little result and undergoing great losses, until they adopted the
> English tactic of bombing civilian residential areas. The great change
> came in the first months of 1943. The Casablanca Conference between
> England and America took place on January 14–23, 1943. It resulted in
> the "Injunctions of Casablanca," that is the decision to heighten the
> bombing of German towns in order to break the spirit of the population.
> This was a deliberate breach of international law on the part of the two big
> democracies, a *unilateral violation* [emphasis added] of the law forbidding
> attacks on civilian populations.
>   Goebbels raved in the Berliner Sportpalast: "If it's total war you want,
> if it has to be more total and more radical, then it will be, and so much
> more radical and so much more total than anything you can imagine
> today." This is how the two big democracies suppressed international law,
> hand in hand with the brown tyranny. The crimes of Nazi Germany are
> known, but those of the conquerors are not.

Here, the author lists the air raid attacks on German towns, Japanese
towns and the atomic bombings: "After the war, a Military Tribunal
was held at Nuremberg by the victors, to deal with war crimes committed by those whom they had conquered, whereas it was impossible to
deal with war crimes committed by their own subjects. Consequently

however, the Principles of Nuremberg were drawn up and today they form an integral part of international law."

This text, with its reference to Goebbels, not only grossly deforms the facts of history, making no mention, for example, of Coventry, which was bombed in April of 1941, or of the bombing of London, Rotterdam, and other places. It also contains nothing suggesting that these bombings could be considered as an effect of National Socialism, let alone as a punishment. The blame is projected onto the allied Anglo-Saxon nations, which are assimilated to unpunished war criminals while the extermination of the Jews is passed over in silence. The Conference of Casablanca was held in 1943. In 1943, Auschwitz was at the height of its activity. It would seem that we have here a text setting out the arguments of National Socialism as they were proferred at the time and as we find them reproduced and, I hasten to add, refuted, in the writings of Thomas Mann.

I have examined this ahistorical mode of thinking, this inability to differentiate between the effect and the cause, the "before" and the "after," the "how" and the "why" elsewhere. I shall not return to the subject here, although I do feel that it is linked to the very essence of totalitarian "madness."

I once asked Hillel Klein, a well-known Israeli analyst who was deported to a concentration camp and who has given many lectures in Germany, if he had any explanation for the widespread development and intensity of the pacifist movement in Germany. He replied, "They are afraid the fire of Heaven will be sent down upon them." In the light of the documents quoted above, I accept this simple explanation as satisfactory enough. It has the merit too of avoiding discussions centering around pacifism as such, while replying, at least in part, to the question: why Germany? The explanation usually given by the Germans, that they would be the first to be annihilated, does not stand up to close examination. Only 250 kilometers separate France from the East German border, where the SS 20 missiles are installed. One must therefore conclude that an atomic war would also destroy France.

During World War II, the spirit of absolute Evil was in Germany—another theme frequently found in the broadcasts of Thomas Mann. It did not become possible to feel any sympathy for the German civilians until the war was over. In Nazi-occupied Europe, the bombing of Germany was seen as the promise that deliverance was at hand. And this, surely, was the purpose of the bombings. Had the atomic bomb been perfected earlier on, who, *at that time,* would have found it illegitimate to use it on Germany? In all probability Germans are aware of this, at least on a certain level.

It is extremely difficult to be—or even to have been—the object of such hatred, and to know that you have incarnated (and not just represented) absolute Evil at the time when, as Thomas Mann has put it, Faust allied himself with the Devil.

How is it possible to face such guilt? Few are able to bear up against it other than in the form of *persecutory* guilt.

Thus we find the Green Movement, bypassing the guilt associated with the Luftwaffe air raids by projecting the fault onto the allied Anglo-Saxon nations, and freeing themselves in the process of the most terrible guilt, the guilt of the genocide, the final solution, in the light of which Nazism becomes a unique case amongst the dozens of fascist regimes that have existed and still exist throughout the world.

In Germany, one speaks of a *nuclear holocaust,* and references to it are more frequent than elsewhere.

The proposition I should like to make is that the German obsession with being destroyed by the atomic bomb is, in fact, a *resurgence of the final solution* of which they would become the victims this time: *Die Entlösung der deutschen Frage.*

If then German pacifism is, at least in part, the expression of anxiety, the measure of which can be gauged from the photos of pacifist demonstrations, with their figures clad in garments portraying skeletons, or gigantic clocks pointing at five to the countdown bringing the end of the world (these representations call to mind certain symbols of German romanticism, the blind dials of Eternity in Jean-Paul, for example), and if this anxiety constitutes a form of persecutory guilt, what about the other themes of the Green Movement, and in what way are these related to the anxiety generated by fear of the final solution?

THE THEME OF ECOLOGY

Here I would like to take a few preliminary precautions. I am indeed aware that the forests of Europe are in real danger, and German forests particularly so. I am also convinced that we have to protect our water, air and food supplies and to keep a tight control on the toxic substances and drugs that are in use today. I am actively committed to the fight for the protection of animals; I oppose vivisection and peace is dear to me. It is not my intention to question the validity of the causes the Green Movement in Germany is defending. On the whole I agree with them. But once again I wonder what explanation can be found for their intensity, the heatedness, the excessiveness, the violence in Germany? When the cause is peace, why this new alliance with the spirit of National Socialism as evidenced in the indecent Nuremberg Tribunal II?

"Herr Professor, somebody has lit a cigarette. At the first puff, thick yellowy-blue smoke pours from his mouth. What are you thinking about? 'Nicotine', 'tar products', coronary arteries, or the cremation of Indian widows? I'm thinking of chimneys myself, particularly big ones, square and rough-and-ready, and the stench of them . . ." says Rudi to Liberé in *Schwarzer Schwann*.

"You've got to take a machete, you've got to cut the fumes that are seeping in, cut it through to let the air in. There must be some breathable air somewhere," Frau Liberé says. And then again: "The smell of Benares, reeking steam; on the banks, men, blackened by soot, prodding their iron stakes into the pyre. All around there are bones, and ashes, three feet high. And what's the reason for it all? To mollify the spirits of the dead. As if every human alive had a bad conscience . . ."

In the Green pamphlets under the heading "Luft" (air), I find endless repetitions of these more or less explicit evocations of the cremation ovens and the gas chambers, where one tries in desperation, and to the point of exhaustion, to find some "breathable air" in the heights. In the pamphlet describing a "Programm für Hamburg," for example, one finds:

> The air of Hamburg is full of particles of dust in suspension which contain oxides that produce acids when, as is likely, they penetrate the lungs, precipitates of heavy metal dust and hydrogen carbo-oxides which are part carcinogenic and fluorine contaminated. We only escaped "smog" in the second half of January owing to favorable climatic conditions. The normal level of air pollution has reached the point where, in the long run, it can only result in devastating damage. Rather than enforcing measures to desulphur at least 90 percent of waste gas—this is feasible from the technical point of view—Federal legislative action against "emission" has succeeded only in obtaining a "more equitable distribution" of the poisons by a heightening of chimneys. [. . .] In certain areas, the concentrations of noxious substances require very precise measurement.
>
> The GAL calls for immediate action to cleanse the air of pollution by all the most modern technology available for the protection of the environment. We demand:

- that Hamburg be immediately declared a zone threatened by air pollution;
- that immediate steps be taken to pressure HEW into installing filtering equipment against gas fumes in all electric power plants;
- that all possible legal action be brought against industrial pollutors (chemical factories, refineries, blast-furnaces) to obtain the installation of additional technological equipment designed to protect the environment;
- the immediate publication of reports drawn up by scientific experts whose task it will be to conduct a study of air conditions in Hamburg (dust toxicity, the combined action of the various noxious substances; the creation of programs to measure certain particularly noxious substances such as heavy metal residues, for example, solutions of hydrogen carbo-oxides; the increased use of bio-indicators);
- the immediate creation of a cadastre conducting surveys of emissions;
- the lowering of the "smog" alarm level and the compilation of a catalogue of measures for this purpose;
- a total ban on the production and use of asbestos;
- an immediate halt to the escape of waste gas from refineries.

On page 6 of *Die Grünen: Das Bundesprogramm,* under the title "Economy and the Working World," there is a striking photograph of factory chimneys vomiting a thick black smoke that is very reminiscent of the cremation ovens.

On page 25 of the same brochure, one finds the following lines:

In the Federal Republic, gigantic amounts of waste gas and dust are projected into the air, such as carbon monoxide, sulfur dioxide, called suffocating oxide (sic) and carbon hydroxide, as well as dust and soot. Thousands of people have already fallen victim to catastrophes brought about by fog. The combined action of the different noxious substances (synergism) and the accumulation of poison through the food chains, lead to an increase in the health hazards that endanger human life. [. . . We demand] the immediate enforcement of an effective set of measures curbing the discharge of noxious substances by industrial complexes and sources of power (electric power plants), cars and airplanes, waste incinerators, public and private heating appliances, the violent exhaust given off by cars; petrol free of benzol and lead [. . .]; a total ban on the distribution and evacuation of all carcinogenic toxic substances; the speedy publication of reports on the harmful effects of air pollution by toxic substances (the threat of cancer).

In order to reduce the quantities of exhaust gas discharged into the atmosphere, filtering apparatus, built into the vehicle itself, should be made obligatory.

In the film *Shoah* (1985), director Claude Lanzmann gets Franz Schalling (Germany) to speak. He asks him:

"Describe the gas lorries."
"Big trucks."
"Very big?"
"Hum . . . Let's see . . . from here to the window. Just furniture removal vans with two doors at the back.
"How did it work? How, what was used to kill?"
"The exhaust gases."
"The exhaust gases?"
"It was like this: One of the Poles shouted Gas! Then the driver climbed under the truck, to fix the pipe through which the gas passed to the inside of the vehicle, gas from the motor."
"How did the gas penetrate inside?"
"Through a narrow pipe. A shaft. He fiddled with something under the truck, but I don't really know what."

Certainly there is a hard core of truth in the accusations that pollution of the atmosphere damages the forest, living creatures and the architecture of cities, and this is what lends credibility to the unconscious staging of a scene where the specters of the past make their reappearance.[7] As a matter of fact, the world of the Green movement, the "alternative" universe, is called "die Szene," that is, the stage. At this point I must mention the "cult of nature," so much a part of Germany from the romantic period on and backcloth to the Green Movement (see the following chapter, "The Paradox of the Freudian Method"). The Green movement is said to have six million dues-paying members.

Add to the above a concern for the aged, the disabled, the mentally ill, the fight against vivisection, and you have a certain number of attitudes and aims which run counter to the horrors of Nazism, where euthanasia was the fate of the disabled and of psychotics, and where Nazi physicians experimented on deported prisoners. Add also the struggle to put an end to discrimination against gypsies and homosexuals. A great campaign is being conducted by the Green Movement in favor of the Third World. The aim is to fight for the rights of those populations which had previously been labelled inferior races. Nazi values have been inverted. The brochures of the Green Movement are full of photographs of men, gaunt with hunger, and children with immense eyes and bony bodies recalling only too vividly the prisoners who were discovered on the liberation of the concentration camps.[8] However, these brochures do not mention the gulag or the internment of Russian dissidents in psychiatric hospitals. Neither do they say anything about Afghanistan or Poland (at least in the dozen or so brochures that I happened to read.)

In a situation of persecutory guilt, it seems that a subject, who feels he is the bearer of Evil, must project this Evil onto the person he takes to represent Good, as opposed to Evil, in order to eliminate the distance that separates the two protagonists. This distance represents the difference between Good and Evil and constitutes, of necessity, a permanent accusation. The object, then, is to vitiate the person who resembles you the least. It can be supposed that the same process takes place where nations are concerned. Inasmuch as one still harbors unconscious feelings of guilt for the horrors of Nazism, this Evil is not projected onto the power which does indeed have features in common with Nazism (totalitarianism and the universe of concentration camps) but onto the one which resembles Nazism the least, whatever its imperfections and misdeeds may be.[9] Moreover, America actually dropped the atomic bomb on a country which was allied to the Nazis.

Hiroshima, the records of the Nuremberg Tribunal II tell us, is directly linked to the bombings of German cities. Thus persecutory guilt sets the scenery: a concentration camp—attacked by "suffocating" gas coming from car exhausts or pouring from huge factory chimneys in thick clouds of smoke—under threat of imminent nuclear "holocaust."

In this respect, it should be noted that *the Jews are never mentioned* in the brochures of the Green Movement. A strange silence reigns over the Jewish question. Mechanisms which I cannot examine within the framework of this chapter explain this silence.[10] But the most important point, it seems to me, is that the Germans have taken the place of the Jews in this world; at least that is the unconscious meaning of the play being performed on the stage of the Green Theater.

We are faced with the effects of a guilt that leads a certain number of Germans to an unconscious identification with those who had been the victims of their parents, or possibly their grandparents. The distorted, mutilated, censored past is actualized: it is here and now that the total catastrophe is about to take place, in "flame and smoke and blood" to quote the prophetic poem by Heinrich Heine "The Twilight of the Gods," written in 1823–24.

CONCLUSION

The question is, can such a persecutory guilt be worked through, i.e., can it be changed into a depressive guilt and overcome? It is obvious that on the individual level we do have certain elements on which to base an answer. It seems that counter-identification to the father is the worst possible solution. It carries the possibility of the return of the repressed, in one form or another. In an analysis, the aim is to help the patient assume all identifications to both parents in the primal scene. For the children of tormentors, as also is the case for the children of victims, the primal scene, represented as the relationship between both protagonists, is a terrifying one because its outcome is the destruction of one of the parents, or their mutual destruction. However, in clinical work, these are identifications that have to be worked through and integrated, not short-circuited. The solution does not lie in favoring reaction formations going against the parents' characters. The energy that makes sublimation possible, and which is necessary for authentic reparation activities, can only be freed at this price. Thus, identification to the parents in one's personal life story, attained only by facing up to depression, is a forerunner of identification to much more impersonal functions, ones that are independent of the actual character traits of the parents (the father essentially, in this context). This is exactly what we find in Thomas Mann's essay "A Brother," where he writes about the attitude one should adopt toward the founder of Nazism: "A brother . . . A rather disagreeable and humiliating brother. It gets on your nerves, it's so very painful a kinship. Nevertheless, I have no wish to close my eyes to him, because recognizing oneself, struggling to unite with what is hateful is, once again, better, more sincere, than hate."

On the level of the masses, we psychoanalysts do not have the answer. Does anyone, in fact? It would be a wise move for the leaders of a great country to act as substitutes for the failing parents, helping their compatriots face all that has been denied, and providing models. There were resisters in Germany. Where are the streets that have been named after them. (There are streets named after Stauffenberg, who was the head of the plot to assassinate Hitler in July 1944, and Thomas Mann, but why not others?) Where are the monuments dedicated to their memory? And G.F. Duckwitz, a German diplomat in Copenhagen who informed the Danish officials in 1943 of the impending deportation of the Jews—will his memory ever be honored?

Some German statesmen have indeed taken steps in this direction: Willy Brandt, when he knelt facing the Warsaw ghetto, the President of the Federal Republic, Von Weisäcker, in the speech he made following Ronald Reagan's visit to Bitburg, Klaus Von Dohnanyi, Mayor of Hamburg, who stressed the specificity of Nazism, as compared to other fascist regimes and enjoined his compatriots to say not only "unser Beethoven," "unser Bach," but also "unser Hitler," in his welcoming speech to the Congress of the International Psycho-Analytical Association in Hamburg. (In Germany one speaks of fascism, not Nazism. In East Germany this makes the phenomenon consistent with the Marxist schema. Fascism can, if necessary, be taken as a variant of capitalism. The genocide is something quite different. For Germans from the West, the use of the word "fascism" instead of "Nazism" places Hitler's regime on a level with those other dictatorships of Mussolini, Salazar, Franco and Pinochet. It evades the very essence of Nazism, that is, an ideology based on racism and carried to its logical end, the "final solution" and the ruling of the world for one thousand years by the Aryans. There is no way of saying anti-Nazi in German. One uses the word "antifascist.") But what of the others who are reluctant to displease their electorate (former Nazis) and hesitant to celebrate the German anti-Nazi resistance, who, can it ever be overlooked, were the ones to go against orders? Even today it is hard to know if they should be honored as heroes or treated as traitors. *Quis custodet custodes?*

POSTSCRIPT

An article written by Elisabeth Brainin and Isidor Kaminer, "Psycho-Analysis and National Socialism,"[11] mentions a slogan that was in use in the protests against the entry of the western highway into Frankfurt: "The Jews were gassed in gas chambers, we are gassed in the street." So worded, this slogan seems to bear out my hypotheses. It is, however, very disconcerting to find that this sudden awareness of one of the main fantasies on which the Green Theater is built does not bring the whole stage toppling down with it. Here, we find some indication of the very nature and the violence of the mechanisms involved and the function filled by ideology (in this case the Green ideology) is brought to light. In cases where a belief is shared by a group, individual reality testing is swept away in favor of the group reality, i.e., its belief. This makes it possible to believe one really is the victim of car exhaust gas in exactly the same way as the Jews were, without bursting into laughter at the scandalous nature of such a statement, or breaking into tears rather, because one can never overestimate the immense grief that the Green illusion must turn into persecution at all costs.

8.

THE PARADOX OF THE FREUDIAN METHOD: FROM THE ABOLISHMENT OF OTHERNESS TO THE UNIVERSAL LAW

To Klaus Von Dohnanyi

Apollonian accounts of what is taking place in the primitive abyss of Dionysos.
Arnold Zweig, "Freud's Odyssey"

Arnold Zweig's definition of Freud's works[1] seems to me to highlight an intrinsic feature of the psychoanalytic method and its paradoxical aspect: the opposition between the subject matter—the unconscious, the primitive abyss of Dionysos, and its project, which in the 1922 edition of the *Encyclopaedia* is defined as threefold:

1. . . . a procedure for the investigation of mental processes which are almost inaccessible by any other means;
2. . . . a method for the treatment of neurotic disorders that has been elaborated on the basis of this investigation;
3. . . . a series of psychological conceptions elaborated in this manner and which are progressively being shaped into a new scientific discipline.

The implication of these three terms, "procedure," "method" and "scientific discipline," is that the three branches of the psychoanalytic "project" call upon logical thought processes. The aim is to direct an Apollonian flood of light into the enigmatic depths of Dionysos.

I use the phrase "psychoanalytic method" in its broadest connotation, meaning the very specific relationship that is established between the analyst, be he or she an investigator of the unconscious, a therapist or a theoretician, and his or her object.

Freud himself restricted the meanings of "psychoanalysis" to two, or even to one. "While it was originally the name of a particular therapeutic method, it has now also become the name of a science—the science of the unconscious mental processes," he says in 1925 in his *Autobiographical Study.*

It is this unprecedented association of the unconscious and science that I wish to examine in greater detail by studying the cultural setting in which Freud put his intellect to work, and, on a deeper level, the way in which this heritage conditioned his attitude toward human phenomena. The papers presented at the 34th Congress of the International Psycho-Analytical Association (Hamburg, 1985) dealing with "The Influence of German-Speaking Culture on the Thought of Freud" doubtless sparked this reflection. I recall that Didier Anzieu (France) and Ernst Ticho (Washington) presented papers which were discussed by Ilse Grübich-Simitis (Discussant, Frankfurt), Peter Neubauer (Moderator, New York) and Eva Laible (Reporter, Vienna).

THE SUBTERRANEAN AND NOCTURNAL FORCES IN GERMAN CULTURE AND THE FREUDIAN VENTURE

In this essay, my intention is to put forth—as others before me have done—the extent to which German culture of the nineteenth century, and essentially Romanticism, has been the scene of a violent upheaval which has shaken art, literature and philosophy, breaking the chains of the narrow prison where the *Aufklärung* had confined the German mind. The themes which came to the fore were the aspiration to attain a state of Nothingness, to merge with Nature, with the boundless universe, to annihilate time and space. Dreams are at the heart of German Romanticism and, as the preromantic writer Karl-Philip Moritz says, the dividing wall separating dream from reality is on the point of crumbling.[2] And it is true that the boundaries between persons, between man and nature, become blurred. In *Anton Reiser* (1786–1790), Moritz writes: "He often used to spend hours looking at a calf, looking at its head, its eyes, its ears, its muzzle; just as he used to study human beings, snuggling up to the animal as close as he could, possessed by the extravagant idea that he could perhaps, by the power of his thought, penetrate into the innermost nature of the beast . . ." The aim in *Anton Reiser* is to break away from one's Ego, to escape from the confines of one's identity, to go beyond one's finitude. "He was as though over-burdened by the weight of his existence. As if, day after day, he had to get up with himself, go to bed with himself, dragging his detested Ego after him at every step . . . The idea that henceforth he would have to be himself, relentlessly, that he would never be another, that he was forever confined within himself by a potent spell . . . this led him bit by bit to the brink of the river." In *The Diary of a Visionary* Moritz writes: "I had no idea of place; I was nowhere and yet everywhere. I felt as if I had been torn away from the chain of objects and no longer needed space." And also:

> At times, I have known a sensation that has frightened me to the inner-most recesses of my soul, despite its very sweetness. In contemplating mighty nature about me, I felt like one lost, who should press heaven and earth to his heart, joining himself in wedlock to this beautiful Whole. This sensation shook me to the depths of my existence; it was as though I longed to lose myself, suddenly dissolved into this Whole, to exist no longer, isolated and foresaken like a flower that withers and dies.

And lastly, in *Andreas Hartknopf* (1785–1790): "The ideas of childhood are like a delicate thread which binds us into the chain of all mortals, conferring on us, to the extent that this is possible, the condition of isolated mortals existing only for themselves. Our childhood would thus be the Lethe from which we have drunk, to keep us from dissolving in the Whole that has been and which is to come, to achieve an individual personality with its correctly defined limits."

This dissolving of the Ego is to be found in almost all German Romantics. In his *Letters on Landscape Painting* (1820) Carus writes: "When Man contemplates the magnificent unity of a landscape, he becomes aware of his own smallness. He loses himself in this infinity, feeling that everything is in God, renouncing his own individual exis-tence." There is, then, a unity, a possible fusion between man, God and Nature. An antireligious idea, a gnostic conception of the world.

In Jean-Paul's writings, one finds frequent evocations of an Ego that observes itself, is afraid of itself, or disappears:

I no longer knew what I was. I was no longer thinking human thoughts. I
was neither sad nor happy. The world had disappeared into the chasm, I
was alone. Something dark and shapeless (though I know not what it was,
nor whether this apparition was not *me gazing at myself*) pressed me to
scan the horizon: within the Nothingness I saw something which could
have been the vibrations of the air before one's eyes, I thought I was seeing
Nothingness itself, playing out its inner struggles [. . .] At last the spectre
rose up from amongst those dream-like things, a dream-like shape itself,
and said to me: "*It is you. I thought of my Ego and shuddered in fright.*"
(Draft of a poetic dream, quoted in A. Béguin.)

The very uncertainty and fragility of the Ego leads Tieck to state:
"Everything that surrounds us is real only up to a certain point."[3]
Heine's description of Hoffman (1833) is of a man who: ". . . felt that
he himself had become a ghost. All nature was to him an imperfect
mirror, in which he saw, distorted in a thousand ways, the cast of his
own dead face; and his works were naught else than a horrible shriek of
terror in twenty volumes."

Heine also points out that in their relationship to nature, most of the
Romantic poets are mystics who ". . . resembled in many aspects the
devotees of India, who dissolve in Nature and at last begin to feel as if
they and Nature were one."

The Romantics and the philosophers of Nature believe in a cosmic
unity, in a great primeval Whole. Nature is an infinite cycle where each
individual existence is meaningless except in relation to this gigantic
whole. There is no death, because dying is merely a return to the womb
of nature whence one is recreated is another form (an idea which per-
vades the works of Sade). Every element is a fragment of the unity that
has been lost. One strives to find this unity again, to become part of the
universal harmony and to retrieve the powers which were ours before
the separation, before the Fall.

Heine considers *Naturphilosophie,* the German idealistic philosophy
and Romanticism, with the latter's penchant for the Middle Ages and
folklore, uniting them into one striking all-encompassing vision which
he compares to a revival of ancient German pantheism. He writes in
Religion v. Philosophy in Germany:

Our first Romanticists were, in fact, moved by a pantheistic instinct,
which they did not themselves comprehend. The sentiment, which they
mistook for a yearning towards the Catholic mother Church, was of
deeper origin than they suspected [. . .] I must here recall what was said in

the first part of this book, where I showed how Christianity absorbed the elements of the old Germanic religion—how after undergoing the most outrageous transformation, these elements were preserved in the popular beliefs of the Middle Ages in such a way that the old worship of nature came to be regarded as mere wicked sorcery, the old gods as odious demons, and their chaste priestesses as profligate witches.[4] [. . .] They wished to restore the Catholicism of the Middle Ages, for they felt that in this Catholicism there still survived many sacred recollections of their first ancestors, many splendid memorials of their earliest national life.

My purpose here, in dealing at such length with this Romantic yearning for union with Nature, mystical ecstasy (and in passing I should at least mention Novalis and Hölderlin), and a return to pantheism, is to stress the nature of the terrain on which the most beautiful flowers of Romanticism have grown, and especially those which are of interest to us as analysts—the passion for dreams, mental pathology and the unconscious. These have their roots in the fusion with the mother.

The father, in his role as the third person who separates the mother from the child, has disappeared. God and Nature are one. Thomas Mann, who only mentions Heine once, in *The Genesis of a Novel* where he says: "During this period I was reading a great deal of Heine: the essays on German philosophy and literature, and his piece on the Faust legend as well," shares this interpretation. As early as 1930, we find it in Mann's "An Appeal to Reason" (in *The Order of the Day*,) in which he speaks of "a new mental attitude" which followed the French Revolution, and its celebration of "the darkness of the soul, the Mother-chthonic, the holy procreative underworld." He speaks also of "this nature-religion, by its very nature inclining to the orgiastic and to bacchic excess." In "Europe Beware" (1935), he uses almost the same terms to describe the "intellect which has turned on itself [. . .] and then denied itself in favour of life and life-giving forces, of the unconscious, the dynamic, the darkly creative, the earth-mother, the holy and creative underworld." This time, however, he is clearly referring to National Socialism, which he associates with German Romanticism (a theme to which I shall return). Thomas Mann feels that "the love of nature" is inherent to the German character ("Germany and the Germans", 1945). In the same essay he speaks again of Romanticism: "The Germans are the people of the romantic counter-revolution." The words referring to the fusion with the primitive mother are there again when he speaks of a "certain dark richness and piousness—I might say:

antiquarianism of soul which feels very close to the chthonian, irrational and demonic forces of life."

As early as January 1926, in a lecture Mann gave in France, "Les tendances spirituelles de l'Allemagne d'aujourd'hui" (in *Cahiers de l'Herne*) he defines Germans as "the people of Goethe," adding that:

> We can never make an exclusive cult of primitive and chaotic powers at the expense of the powers of light and order unless we deny the moral and educative impressions we have received from him, and in the long run, this is an indefensible position. [. . .] The powers of Chaos and the *Earth-Mother* [emphasis added], the procreative sources of life, were familiar to him, and he was careful not to deny them. He recognized them as sacred but never consented to worship them as divine. For him it was the powers of the day, of Light and of Reason, which were divine.

For Thomas Mann, Goethe can be compared to "those godlike warriors who conquered the dragon and chaos."

As Albert Béguin has shown in his classic book, *L'Ame romantique et le rêve. Essai sur le romantisme allemand et la poésie française* (1937), the dream is accorded a very central place in German Romanticism, and I would feel embarrassed to speak on this subject before an audience which is immersed in a culture that is probably permeated by this theme. At the Hamburg Congress, my French colleagues, Henri and Madeleine Vermorel, presented an individual paper in which they quoted passages on the subject of the dream and the unconscious from philosophical and literary works of the Romantic period, and especially from the writings of Von Shubert, Lichtenberg, Novalis, Schleiermacher, Schegel, Schelling, Fichte, Jean-Paul Richter, et al., on the basis of which they felt justified in entitling their contribution "Freud, a Romantic?"—though they chose to put it as a question.

It is an indisputable fact that German Romanticism has thrown new light on the depths of the human soul. This movement of liberation has brought the unconscious out into the open, somewhat like those surface mines that hardly need to be excavated to reveal the wealth buried below. The primal processes have won supremacy over the secondary ones. The liberation, as I hope I have shown, calls for a union with the mother and the eradication of the paternal universe. Testifying to this disappearance of the father, we find an indiscrimination between God and Nature ("Mother Nature") and a more or less total defeat of Reason. In my essay "The Archaic Matrix of the Oedipus Complex" (in this volume), I set out to show the existence of a primary desire to discover a universe without obstacles, without roughness or differences, entirely smooth, identified with the mother's belly stripped of its contents, an interior to which one has free access. It is my opinion that behind this desire, which implies the elimination of the father, his attributes, his representants and his products—the children—one finds a more basic and more archaic wish, of which the return to the smooth maternal belly is the representation. It is a question, in fact, of rediscovering on the level of thought, a mental functioning without hindrances, with psychic energy flowing freely. Father (and his derivatives) represent reality. They have to be destroyed so that the mode of mental functioning which is proper to the pleasure principle, may be recovered, i.e., the primary processes. Referring to Freud's article on "The two principles of mental functioning" (1911), I have shown that thought is linked to the reality principle—and therefore to the paternal universe—and that it can be violently fought against, destroyed even, in order to regain access to the smooth maternal belly. Thought then begins to function, in certain respects, according to the pleasure principle and the laws of the primary processes. The result is a total confusion of values, a return to chaos and anomie. Reason is a representative of the Father and of the Law. Its decline, a sign that the father has been defeated, indicates that a process of merging with the archaic mother is taking place. This is why I do not think that Freud was a Romantic. That was certainly not his wish, and moreover, had he simply been a Romantic, he would have steeped himself in the unconscious and set up its cult. He would have been a poet, an ideologist, or a dissident psychoanalyst. He would not have created psychoanalysis. The Freudian enterprise is not a celebration of the Unconscious. Freud sought to subdue the nocturnal, subterranean powers that so strongly pervade German culture, not to delight in them. The fact is that the place of the father, and thence of Reason, is fundamental to the Freudian venture and to the psychoanalytic method.

THE ROLE OF JEWISH CULTURE IN THE THOUGHTS OF FREUD

Certain statements by Freud, setting out his hopes for the role to be accorded to Reason, are very well-known. "Our best hope for the future is that intellect—the scientific spirit, reason—may in the process of time establish a dictatorship in the mental life of man," he says in his *New Introductory Lectures*: "A Weltanschauung?" (1933), a gloomy year for expressing such a hope.

In 1927, in *The Future of an Illusion*, he declares:

> We may insist as often as we can that man's intellect is powerless in comparison with his instinctual life, and we may be right in this. Nevertheless, there is something peculiar about this weakness. The voice of the intellect is a soft one, but it does not rest till it has gained a hearing. Finally, after a countless succession of rebuffs, it succeeds. This is one of the few points on which one may be optimistic about the future of mankind, but it is in itself a point of no small importance.

Here, Freud casts Reason in a role which requires it to act in accordance with its own laws, the laws of the reality principle: to resign itself to waiting. This victory will, however, certainly materialize, but in the long run. It is hard to imagine that such a victory will ever be definitive and permanent, but this optimistic statement is consistent with the spirit of the Enlightenment to which Freud claimed he was heir. And so convinced was he of his heritage that essential references to German Romanticism have been omitted in his writings. The first chapter of *Civilization and its Discontents* (1929) illustrates this point. Freud discusses the "oceanic feeling" of Romain Rolland, describing what, to this latter, would be a "sensation of 'eternity', a feeling of something limitless, unbounded as it were, 'oceanic' [. . .] That is to say, it is a feeling of an indissoluble bond, of being one with the world as a whole." Since Romain Rolland considers that this feeling is at the origin of the need for religion, Freud refers it to the "longing for the father," although only a few pages prior to this he had associated it with the primary ego-feeling of the infant whose relationship with the father is problematic. In any case, to Freud, the whole issue seems "wrapped in obscurity" and he confesses that he finds it "very difficult to work with these almost intangible quantities." He makes allusions to trances and ecstasy and then closes the subject by saying: ". . . but I am moved to exclaim in the words of Schiller's diver: *Let him rejoice who breathes up here in the roseate light!*"

When this feeling of union with the world as a whole is such a permanent feature of German Romantic literature, is it not striking to find it attributed, as something quite new, to Romain Rolland? And is it not striking to find, too, that in total opposition to all we have just said about Romantic pantheism which has the mother for object, Freud is only able to refer the need for religion to the father? And lastly, is it not striking to find Freud maintaining that a state such as this, involving the eradication of the Father and the return to the maternal womb, is unknown to him, and not desired?

It would seem that there is a "repressed" part in Freud, composed of all his ties to the Romantic dimension of German culture. Freud is very much a Jew in this respect. The paternal dimension is intrinsic to Judaism. The importance of the father in psychoanalysis begins with the fundamental role that the death of his father played in Freud's self-analysis, as Didier Anzieu has shown in *L'Auto-analyse de Freud* (1975). It continues with the place accorded to the Oedipus complex, which Freud often calls the "paternal complex" and its role as the "core complex" in neuroses, religion and social institutions (*Totem and Taboo,* 1913). It is coupled with what I have named the *separation* principle. I take the liberty here of repeating certain reflections that are presented in my article "Perversion and the Universal Law" (1982–1984) in *Creativity and Perversion.* I examined a number of biblical commandments taken from the *Manuel d'Instruction religieuse Israëlite* by the Grand Rabbi Deutsch (1977) listed under the heading "The forbidden mixture." First we find the well-known commandment: "Thou shalt not seethe a kid in its mother's milk." An article by M. Wulff, entitled "Prohibition against Simultaneous Consumption of Milk and Flesh in Orthodox Jewish Law" (1945) points out that seething the kid in its mother's milk was a part of the rites in the worship of Astarte: ". . . seething the kid in his mother's milk means placing the child back in its mother's belly, giving it to the full and individual possession of the mother. The son belongs to the mother." Wulff's thesis is that this biblical commandment should be seen as an *attempt to destroy matriarchal law.* Matriarchal law, we know, represents a fusion between mother and child, and excludes the father, the mediator. The quality of *isolation* characterizing Jewish ritual eating habits—particularly the strict separation of flesh and milk in all food—may be traced back to the days when the people of Israel, at that time a small tribe of shepherds beset by paganism, struggled to uphold Jewish monotheism, a struggle that was also of an intrapsychic nature.

In *Leviticus* 19:19, the Lord says: "Ye shall keep my statutes. Thou shalt not let thy cattle gender with a diverse kind: thou shalt not sow thy field with mingled seed: neither shall a garment mingled of linen and woollen come upon thee."

In *Leviticus* 18:6–18, the Lord lays down the commandments connected more specifically with incest. It is important to note that the aim of these commandments is to maintain the barriers separating one thing from another and preserving the very essence of each of them.

> 6. None of you shall approach to any that is near of kin to him, to uncover their nakedness: I am the Lord.
> 7. The nakedness of thy father, or the nakedness of thy mother, shalt thou not uncover: she is thy mother; thou shalt not uncover her nakedness:
> 8. The nakedness of thy father's wife shalt thou not uncover; it is thy father's nakedness.

The text continues in this manner, evoking every possible variation on this theme of the prohibition of incest, the rythmic incantation of each verse seemingly encircling each case and accentuating the inexorability of the separation.

All these biblical laws are based on a principle of *division* and *separation*. This principle is found at the heart of obsessional neurosis, in the defense mechanism called *isolation*. Significant in this respect is that Freud compared religion to obsessional neurosis ("Obsessive Actions and Religious Practices", 1907); a comparison which is correct where the Jewish religion is concerned. Freud was, however, far too steeped in Judaism, despite being an atheist, ever to imagine that other religions could be devoid of this absolute precept to separate, divide and isolate, or that it might be less all-pervading in other religions. In the Jewish religion this precept also concerns the separation between God and man. God must not be seen (God says to Moses in Exodus 33:20: "Thou canst not see my face: for there shall no man see me, and live.") His name must not be pronounced. He must not be represented. He is unknowable.[5] The idea of entering into a "communion" with God is unthinkable. Mystical effusion, ecstasy, are contrary to the spirit of the Jewish faith because they imply a union with God. There is no natural bond between God and man, only a covenant. God is transcendent, the Truly Other. Indeed, a God with whom one merges loses his paternal character. In *Genesis,* the Creation is based on the principles of distinction, separation and differentiation: "In the beginning God created the Heaven and the Earth. And the Earth was without form and void . . ." God then brings order into this original chaos, dividing it:

". . . and God divided the Light from the Darkness . . . God said, Let there be a Firmament in the midst of the waters and let it divide the waters from the waters. And God made the Firmament and divided the waters which were under the Firmament from the waters which were above the Firmament . . ."

In my earlier essay I pointed out that the original meaning of *nomos* (the law, in Greek) is: "that which is divided up into parts." A further meaning of *nomos* (the accent being on the second syllable) is "division of land," "province," "pasture," "grazing land." Thus, we see that *separation is the foundation upon which Law is built,* or to put it in other words, separation and Law (in the moral as well as in the juridical sense of the word) are one and the same thing. Anything bringing about a separation is to be considered as a representation of the father who prevents the infant from returning to the mother's womb.

It is my postulation that Freud's attitude to the Unconscious can be attributed to a play of forces which reflect, at least in part, his double culture. (Obviously this is just one of the factors involved. The fact of being a German Jew is not enough.) German Romanticism has brought the Unconscious within his reach, so to speak, but he refuses to let himself be engulfed by it; on the contrary, because of his identification with Judaism, he seeks to pin it down, to master it intellectually. He also refuses to deify the Unconscious, an attitude that also reflects his Judaism and the struggle of the Jewish people against idolatry.

It is common knowledge that Freud and the Surrealists—those revamped Romantics—did not get on together. In a letter to André Breton, Freud wrote that he was incapable of understanding how anyone could be interested in collecting dreams (it could be supposed that he refused to understand such an interest, in view of his own efforts to maintain psychoanalysis within the field of science), and that he had little tolerance for psychotics when not in the exercise of his profession.

Though in the first place resistance to psychoanalysis was encountered in those who clung to their sterile, narrowminded rationalizations, before long psychoanalysis was being sapped from within, in an attempt to drag it away into the magic world of irrationality. Freud's reply to Karl Abraham, who had warned him of Jung, was precisely that "things are much easier for us Jews because we are lacking in all mystical leanings." Henceforth, there will be many a variant on this attempt to divert psychoanalysis into the mystical domain. Thus, it can be said that it is this conjunction of the two cultures which enables Freud to explore the Unconscious—the Mother's body—and to send a flood of light into its dark depths, without lurching himself into the abyss.

The special manner in which the Oedipus complex has been resolved probably plays a decisive role. The interest in the mother's body (the Unconscious) is not given up; it is sublimated in an interest for scientific research whose instruments (through identification with the father) are neither destructive, nor in too great a danger of being destroyed. (Here, however, events in Freud's life intervene: his illness led him not only to formulate his theory on the death instinct but also to write his most important articles on femininity, which he sees as obscure, uncanny, disquieting, as though it lay enveloped in a mournful shadow. In all likelihood this attitude barred the way for other discoveries concerning structures that are not in the field of neurosis and which have become part of the analyst's daily work.) One catches a glimpse of a primal scene in which both parents have the capacity to create life.

PSYCHOANALYSIS AS A RAMPART AGAINST BARBARITY

German Romanticism was considered by two of Germany's greatest writers, with the span of a century between them, as carrying within it the seeds of the Apocalypse.

I am told that Heine's book, *Religion v. Philosophy in Germany* (the first articles composing this work were published in France in 1833) is not liked in Germany, and that Thomas Mann's essays on Germany, written before the Nazis came to power and during the Hitler regime, are not always valued. Yet it seems fitting to be grateful to those whose perspicacity and lucidity enable Germans, and anyone who is interested in the history of civilization, to understand the events of the twentieth century in Germany and, at the same time, in the world.

In a strange and very striking prophecy, Heine did indeed foresee the events to which Romanticism, the *Naturphilosophie,* the idealism of Fichte and of other German philosophers would lead:

> . . . the Philosopher of Nature will be terrible in this, that he has allied himself with the primitive powers of nature, that he can conjure up the demoniac forces of old German pantheism; and having done so, there is

aroused in him that ancient German eagerness for battle [. . .] then will break forth again the ferocity of the old combatants, the frantic Berserker rage whereof Northern poets have said and sung so much. [. . .] and the day will come [. . .] The old stone gods will then arise from the forgotten ruins and wipe from their eyes the dust of centuries, and Thor with his giant hammer will arise again, and he will shatter the Gothic cathedrals. [. . .] When ye hear the trampling of feet and the clashing of arms, ye neighbours' children, ye French, be on your guard, and see that ye mingle not in the fray going on amongst us at home in Germany. It might fare ill with you. [. . .] The thought precedes the deed as the lightning the thunder. German thunder is of true German character: it is not very nimble, but rumbles along somewhat slowly. And come it will, and when ye hear a crashing such as never before has been heard in the world's history, then know that at last the German thunderbolt has fallen. At this commotion the eagles will drop dead from the skies and the lions [. . .] will bite their tails and creep into their royal lairs. There will be played in Germany a drama compared to which the French Revolution will seem but an innocent idyl.

And the hour will come. As on the steps of an amphitheatre, the nations will group themselves around Germany to witness the terrible combat.

As you will remember, Heine concludes this astonishing prophecy with the following reminder to the French: "As ye are, despite your present romantic tendency, a born classical people, ye know Olympus [. . .] ye may behold one goddess, who, amidst such gaiety and pastime, wears ever a coat of mail, the helm on her head and the spear in her hand.

She is the goddess of Wisdom."

It is worth noting that Heine makes no allusion at all to the political writings proper of the poets and philosophers of the Romantic period in Germany, though when one reads these in the light of twentieth-century events, it is clear that they are overtly anticipatory. Consider Fichte's *Deutschheit* for example, in his *Discourses to the German Nation* (1807–1808), and more importantly, the Hegelian concept of the master-slave relationship: the God of the Old Testament represents the "schism" engendered by the opposition between subject and object at its most extreme. God is a "foreign" power, submitting nature and crushing man, his slave, whereas the pagan Greeks lived in a state of harmony with the Whole and knew nothing of transcendence. It follows, therefore, that the conception of the State, which is to be contrary to the master-slave relationship, requires the sacrifice of individual interests in favor of the State, the freedom of each individual being achieved in the freely consented submission of all individuals to the superior interests of the State. One can readily understand that freedom such as this, a return to the "beautiful wholeness" of the Greeks, contains the seeds of totalitarianism, whether politically to the left or to the right. In fact, the sole disappearance of otherness in German Romanticism is indication enough that this gestation forebodes a gloomy future.

As I have already mentioned, Thomas Mann understood that German Romanticism was pregnant with the National Socialist monster. This he explains in his political speeches even before Hitler came to power and throughout the period when he was an anti-Nazi refugee.

In 1930, he delivered his "An Appeal to Reason" (in *The Order of the Day*) in Berlin. The pro-Nazi elements in the audience that had gathered in the Beethovensaal to hear him turned rowdy when he spoke of the celebration of "this darkness of the soul, of the Mother-Chthonic . . . which has gone into the nationalism of our day" and when he voiced his fears concerning:

> . . . its character as a nature-cult distinguished by its absolute unrestraint, its orgiastic, radically anti-humane, frenziedly dynamic character. But when one thinks what it has cost humanity, through the ages, to rise from orgiastic nature-cults, from the service of Moloch, Baal and Astarte, with the barbaric refinements of its gnosticism and the sexual excesses of its divinities, to the plane of a more spiritual worship, one stands amazed at the light-hearted way in which today we repudiate our gains and our liberations.
>
> It may seem daring to associate the radical nationalism of our day with these conceptions from a romanticising philosophy. Yet the association is there, and it must be recognized by those concerned to get an insight into the relation of things.
>
> Fed then, by such intellectual and pseudo-intellectual currents as these, the movement which we sum up under the name of National-Socialism and which has displayed such a power of enlisting recruits to its banner, mingles with the mighty wave—a wave of anomalous barbarism, of primitive, popular vulgarity—that sweeps over the world today.
>
> Everything is possible, everything permitted.

The following year, in "The Rebirth of Decency" (1931) Thomas Mann pursues this theme of affiliation between Romanticism, "national chthonian ideas" and National Socialism, going so far as to say: "The popular philosophical position of Irrationalism . . . is something uniquely German." In "Germany my affliction," the diary he kept throughout 1933 and 1934, this theme is insistent. He speaks of "Reason which advocates the irrational," "the mind that preaches 'the soul' and literature [that] preaches 'blood'" and in speaking of Germany he says: "Rather than fearing chaos, she loves it." We know that chaos is a Romantic theme par excellence. In "Europe Beware" (1935) Thomas Mann speaks of "the vulgarization of great and venerated European ideas by the commercialism of the masses." He goes on to say:

> "To be one with everything that lives!" cries Hölderlin in his 'Hyperion'. "With this phrase virtue discards its harness of wrath and the spirit of man its sceptre, and from the unity of being death disappears, and immanent life, eternal youth, beautify and bless the world." We find the dionysiac experience expressed in these words degraded in the group ecstasy [. . .] in the young marching in step [. . .] The young today love the group, stripped of all personal effort, for its own sake, and care little where it leads them [. . .]. The ecstasy of escape from the I and its burdens is an end in itself, and ideas related to it, such as the state, socialism, the grandeur of the fatherland are more or less subsidiary, secondary, and indeed accidental. The real objective is the ecstasy of freedom from the self, from thought, and especially from morality and reason; and, of course, from *fear* also.

For my part, I have not the slightest hesitation in saying that, in all, it is a question of merging with the mother (of casting off one's Ego in a state of giddy exaltation) by destroying all the representatives of the Father (Reason and Law).

The passages in Thomas Mann's works which refer to this affiliation between Romanticism and National Socialism, the eradication of Reason and the victory of destructive forces, are hardly lacking and I am going to quote him twice more. The first quotation is dated August 1941 and is taken from one of his messages broadcast over the BBC (1940–45) in *Listen Germany*:

> I admit that what we call National Socialism has deep roots in German life. It is a degenerate form of ideas which always carried within themselves the seeds of a terrible corruption, but which were in no way foreign to the old, good Germany, civilised and cultured. They were highly thought of: they bore the name of "Romanticism" and offered the world many attractions. It can be said that now they are at bay, in a desperate situation, and were destined to be so, because they led inevitably to Hitler.

In "Germany and the Germans" written after the war (1945, in *The Order of the Day*), he returns to this theme:

> Goethe laconically defined the Classical as the healthy, the Romantic as the morbid. A painful definition for one who loves Romanticism down to its sins and vices. But it cannot be denied that even in its loveliest, most ethereal aspects where the popular mates with the sublime it bears in its heart the germ of morbidity, as the rose bears the worm; its innermost character is seduction, seduction to death. This is its confusing paradox: while it is the revolutionary representative of the irrational forces of life against abstract reason and dull humanitarianism, it possesses a deep affinity to death, by virtue of its very surrender to the irrational and to the past.

Although the theme of Death is continuously present in German Romanticism itself, the theme of destruction is less permanent. Destruction of the paternal universe is, in fact, a consequence of the desire to merge with the mother, and the fantasy can very well be acted upon without its preceeding stages being presented. Certain Romantics do, however, furnish us with terrifying images of destruction. Moritz, in his *Diary of a Visionary*, writes: "In our efforts *to equal God* we were unable to become creators and so turned ourselves to destruction; we created the other way around, since we were unable to create in the direction of the future. We built ourselves a universe of destruction and then, in sweet self-satisfaction, we contemplated our work in history, in tragedy and in our poems."

Jean-Paul's apocalyptic visions in "The Annihilation" of the beginnings and the end of the world also deserve mention here: "Blocks of mountains that had collapsed, the rubble of hills reduced to dust, fell on all sides; clouds and moons in liquefaction dropped like hailstones. The planets passed like arrows . . . and suns, dragging their earths in their wake, crashed heavily down from the heights. When all was done, there remained nothing more than a cloud of ashes, which hung a long time yet, floating . . ."

In "Freud's Position in the History of Modern Thought," written in 1929, Thomas Mann once more evokes the dangers of a popular corruption of Romanticism, the Romantic vulgate so to speak, just as one could similarly speak of the effects of the Nietzschean vulgate on National Socialism. With remarkable lucidity, he expresses his concern about the rise of the irrational: "We are no longer strangers to the disheartening sight of youthful bodies in gay quick-step, songs issuing from young lips, arms flung in a Roman salute, wasting the fine flight of their youth upon hoary ideas." His advice to the youth of the day is to turn toward psychoanalysis, because in his opinion: "Freud's interest as a scientist in the affective does not degenerate into a glorification of its object at the expense of the intellectual sphere. His anti-rationalism consists in seeing the actual superiority of the impulses over the mind, power for power: not at all in lying down and grovelling before that superiority, or in contempt for mind [. . .] it works in the interest of the triumph it envisages in the future for mind and reason." This seems to echo what Thomas Mann said of Goethe in 1926, when he recognized this latter's familiarity with the "powerful forces of Chaos and the motherland" and his refusal "ever to consent to revere them as divine." Similarly, he writes in the same text: "This idea of humanity determined Goethe's attitude to Romanticism, which was one of disapproval. However seductive it may be as an aesthetic phenomenon, Western Romanticism always poses a threat to the immense, accumulated riches of our species. It is the threat that a devastating and overwhelming flood of the primitive and destructive powers of the Dionysiac and the musical will engulf the world of order and light, the Apollonian kingdom of the plastic . . ." Is he not attributing to Goethe exactly what Arnold Zweig sees as being Freud's great achievement: the balance attained between the two opposing realms of Apollo and Dionysos? Within Freud, the theoretician of the Unconscious coexists with the bold diver. "There is something of the material itself which forces one onwards, deeper into sexual symbolism, exclusivity, courage to deal with the unconscious on terms of complete familiarity," wrote Freud to Pfister in 1910 (in *Psychoanalysis and Faith, The Letters of Sigmund Freud and Oskar Pfister, 1909–1939*).

This happy marriage uniting the realms of Apollo and Dionysos is also that of the olive tree and the fig tree, the two Trees of Eden as Thomas Mann says, the union between the mind and the soul. It is interesting to note that in French at least, one speaks of the "French mind" and the "German soul." The soul is also the privileged possession of Slavs and Russians (the *dousha*).

The paradox of the Freudian psychoanalytic method resides, I feel, in this conjunction of Romantic German culture and the Law of Moses, in the maternal cosmic dimension and the paternal universe of separation. It is this conjunction that leads Thomas Mann to say of the Führer, in

"A Brother" (1935, in *The Order of the Day*): "I have a private suspicion that the élan of the march on Vienna had a secret spring: it was directed at the venerable Freud, the real and actual enemy, the philosopher and revealer of the neuroses, the great disillusioner."

Of course, the barrier opposed by Reason and the Law to the chthonian maternal forces (the tiny Oedipal streams "instead of the great open expanse of water once glimpsed" as the authors of *The Anti-Oedipus* would say) bridles outrageousness, the hubris of man, who does not get over this easily.

Could this not be one of the reasons why the Jew is hated, for giving the world a paternal God, a unique God who is venerated to the exclusion of all others? The legend of Faust is indeed truly German, yet it is also universal. Few men are able to reconcile themselves to the fact that the stars are not within their reach. Very likely this also accounts in part for the resistance encountered by Freudian psychoanalysis. Psychoanalysis was described by Thomas Mann, in "Freud and the Future" in *Nobleness of Spirit* (1936) as being characterized by a spirit of *measure* and modesty. It is true that as psychoanalysts, and as Freud and our friend Heine before us,

> The heavens we can safely leave
> To the angels and the sparrows!

POSTSCRIPT

I had finished writing this chapter when I came across a letter from Freud to Lou-Andrea Salome in 1915, in which he writes: "What interests me is the separation, the division into unities which, without this process, would fuse together into a primordial magma."

Notes

CHAPTER 1: FREUD AND FEMALE SEXUALITY

1. Freud's interpretation of the fallen horse phobia leads him to the scene where Fritzl hurts his foot and bleeds. Freud identifies the fallen horses with Fritzl and Hans's father. He thus arrives at the death-wish rather than the castration-wish.

2. We know (Freud, 1911) that Schreber's mother was absorbed, so to speak, by her husband, who had usurped her maternal functions. In this case, as in all cases of male paranoia, what is significant is the absence of a narcissistic cathexis of femininity.

CHAPTER 3: SUBMISSIVE DAUGHTERS

1. Primary passivity has for its object a body whose image is vague. We are still at the auto-erotic stage, following the terminology of 1914 ("On Narcissism: An Introduction"). When the narcissistic stage is reached and the body—support of the Ego—is more clearly separated from the object, there intervenes the identification of the body proper with a stool taking on the shape of the rectum from which comes the identification with a corpse with its anal characteristics. (Cf. *Memoirs of Schreber.*) The identification of the body with a phallus comes later. It implies the existence of fixations at the Oedipal-genital stage. At the autoerotic stage there can be fantasies of the desire (passive) to be devoured. (Cf. the oral triad by K. Lewin: "sleep; eat; be eaten.") We must also, with reference to the carpet, think of adhesive identification (Esther Bick).

2. From "Homosexuality in Women," in *Feminine Sexuality,* J. Chasseguet-Smirgel et al. London: Virago (1981), p. 189.

3. Cf. Paulette Letarte: "The Ego-Ideal and the Fear of Engulfing" in *Revue Française de Psychanalyse* (1973), 37:1134–1135.

4. We must remember that in "The Gospel According to Matthew" Pasolini, in the last part of the film, gave the part of Mary to his own mother. The fantasy of being devoured is referred to by Dominique Fernandez, who connects it with a postcard sent by the father, then in Africa, showing a man being torn to pieces

by a tiger. The theme of cannibalism is found in several of his films. Pasolini had sexual relations near the Rome slaughterhouse with boys working there. Is is not possible to equate this desire to be devoured with the identification with Christ and with the sacrifice of the Mass: "This is my body: this is my blood"?

CHAPTER 4: ON TRANSFERENCE LOVE IN THE MALE

1. *Tringler* in vulgar French means "to make love" ("fuck"). The word *aubépine* ("hawthorn") is very nice. It suggests the dawn (*aube*) and whiteness (from the Latin *albus* or *alba*) and thorns (*épines*). But *pine* is also a vulgar word for "penis." We see here the extent of the psychic work deployed to transform the sexual act into a poetic act without depriving it of its sensuality, as in certain songs from French folklore (I am thinking here of "*Aux marches du palais*", where the little shoemaker describes the sexual act to his beloved, the princess, in exquisite metaphors:

Aux quatre coins du lit (bis)	At the four corners of the bed (bis)
Un bouquet de violettes (lon-la)	A bunch of violets (lon-la)
Un bouquet de violettes	A bunch of violets
Dans le mitan du lit (bis)	In the middle of the bed (bis)
La rivière est profonde (lon-la)	The river is deep (lon-la)
La rivière est profonde	The river is deep
Tous les chevaux du roi (bis)	All the king's horses (bis)
Viennent y boire ensemble (lon-la)	Come to drink there together (lon-la)
Viennent y boire ensemble	Come to drink there together
Et nous y dormirons (bis)	And there we shall sleep (bis)
Jusqu'à la fin du monde (lon-la)	Until the end of the world (lon-la)
Jusqu'à la fin du monde.	Until the end of the world.

2. I believe Freud wrote his major studies on femininity in parallel with his discovery of the death instinct. If his last theory of instincts has been linked with his cancer, should we not also link his theory of femininity with the deadly disease from which he was suffering? The traces of his fear of death are obvious, for example, in "Some psychical consequences of the anatomical distinction between the sexes" (1925): "Time before me is limited," etc.

3. In particular, B. Grunberger in *Narcissism* (New York: International Universities Press, 1979; French edition 1971).

4. "The 'Uncanny,'" 1919.

5. Cf. H. Segal, *A Psycho-analytical Approach to Aesthetics*, 1953.

6. In France, Béla Grunberger has dealt with anality and sadism in his book on narcissism (*Le Narcissisme*, Paris: Payot, 1971 and *Narcissism*, New York: IUP, 1979) and in several of his papers and especially in his "Study of Anal Object Relations" (1960). In the United States, Leonard Shengold has recently published a remarkable article on this topic, stressing the defensive aspect of anality ("Defense Anality and Anal Narcissism," in *Intern. J. of Psycho-Anal.*, 1985,

66:47–73). As Béla Grunberger, Shengold seems to consider anality as forming an important dimension of the mind.

CHAPTER 5: THE ARCHAIC MATRIX OF THE OEDIPUS COMPLEX

1. "The importance of Symbol-Formation in the Development of the Ego" (1930), in *Contributions to Psycho-analysis* (London: The Hogarth Press, 1948), p. 236–250.
2. "Psychotherapy of Psychoses" 1930, p. 251.
3. "The First Stages of the Oedipus Complex and the Formation of the Superego," 1932, *Psychoanalysis of Children*.
4. Otto Rank, *The Trauma of Birth*, Harper Torchbook, 1973.
5. Sigmund Freud, *Inhibitions, Symptoms and Anxiety* (1926), p. 138.
6. Freud undoubtedly refers here to "Thalassa: A Theory of Genitality." New York: *The Psychoanalytic Quarterly*, 1938.
7. Freud, *Inhibitions, Symptoms and Anxiety*, p. 139.
8. Freud, *Inhibitions, Symptoms and Anxiety*, p. 139.
9. See J. Chasseguet-Smirgel, "A Metapsychological Study of Perversion."

CHAPTER 6: THE ARCHAIC MATRIX OF THE OEDIPUS COMPLEX IN UTOPIA

1. The projects which gave birth to the United States are not, in my opinion, utopias, properly speaking. They set out to find the solution to concrete problems and are far from being abstract and idealized wishful thinking even if dreams have their part in them.
2. Jean Servier, *History of Utopia*, Paris Idées/Gallimard, 1967.
3. December 1985: A little book on Nazism (Berstein, S: Le *Nazisme*, Paris: M.A., 1985) speaks of Walter Darré, the "inventor" of the "Blut und Boden" theory: "These conceptions of "blood and soil" led him to be interested in peasantry in which he saw the principle of the conservation of a pure and healthy race, in opposition to cities, considered as the source of the decay of races."
4. In July, 1985, at the Hamburg Congress, when he discussed the papers on the Nazi phenomenon, Mortimer Ostow presented a remarkable text on Nazism viewed in the perspective of the Apocalypse.

CHAPTER 7: "THE GREEN THEATER"

1. Translator's note: This is a reference to Max Ophul's film *The Sorrow and the Pity* (1970), set in France during the Nazi occupation and depicting the different attitudes adopted by the French at that time.

2. See my studies on the examination dream, particularly in *The Ego Ideal* (1985), and *Creativity and Perversion* (1984), London: Free Association Books; New York: Norton.

3. A strange prophecy indeed. In fact, there has not, I think, been one single Jewish bombing in Germany since the end of the war. What other community has so totally refrained from exacting vengeance? And to speak of facts that are close to my heart, because I am French and an analyst, those who have been most actively engaged in the reconciliation between France and Germany, excluding the politicians, are three Jews: Raymond Aron, Alfred Grosser and Joseph Rovan. As for the reconstitution and the reintegration of German psychoanalysis, this has been accomplished almost exclusively by Jewish analysts.

4. Sandoz, G. (1980) *Ces Allemands qui ont défié Hitler,* Paris, Pygmalion, p. 108.

5. This book is detested by the "Grünen" (the Green Movement). One of the pamphlets put out by the GAL (Grün-Alternative Liste) refers to "André Glücksmann's aesthetics of deterrance and his transformation of the image of the imperialist world."

6. The author seems (or wants) to ignore what this day meant for Europe, as if a new English Prime Minister had been nominated "by chance" on this day, the day Belgium and Holland were invaded.

7. One reads reports in the press of panic reactions in Germany following the Chernobyl disaster and it is said that a number of German women have asked to have abortions performed. Whether right or wrong, the question is, why in Germany?

8. In her book *Le vertige allemand* [German Vertigo] (1985, Paris: Olivier Orban), Brigitte Sauzay collects a certain number of "green" themes in this same way. It is difficult to guess if she only has a slight suspicion of what I am trying to get at here, or whether she has really understood. This interesting book was given a very ironic review in *Der Spiegel.*

9. It is interesting to note that in the wake of the Chernobyl disaster there have been no anti-Soviet demonstrations in Germany. On the contrary, in a distorted way, this event has been turned against the United States (cf. Alfred Grosser, "L'atome, la peur, et la raison," in *Le Monde,* May 22, 1986).

10. Of course Israel is the object of attacks, and Joschka Fisher's book, *On the subject of Green Power and its Magnificence* (1984) (Hamburg: Rowohlt) places a photograph captioned "The Massacre of Palestinians in the camps of Sabra and Chatila by Israeli soldiers" opposite the well-known photograph of a Jewish child wearing a cap and holding its hands up, taken in the Warsaw ghetto in 1944. Thus the balance is restored. The Israelis are no different to the Nazis and Sabra and Chatila are the equivalent of the Warsaw ghetto. It is perhaps worth mentioning that the Christians and not the Israelis perpetrated these massacres. The Israelis were accused only of having failed to foresee the massacres.

11. In *Ecrits du Temps* (1984), No. 6, translated from the German review *Psyche,* November 1982.

CHAPTER 8: THE PARADOX OF THE FREUDIAN METHOD

1. In *Die psychoanalytishe Bewegung*, 4th year, March–April 1932, No. 2. Quoted by Marthe Robert in the Preface to *Sigmund Freud–Arnold Zweig, Correspondance, 1927–1939*, Paris: Gallimard, 1973.

2. *The Diary of a Visionary*, 1790, quoted in A. Béguin (1939).

3. R. Minder (1936) *Ludwig Tieck*.

4. Here we see the origin of a phrase Freud repeated many a time: "The gods of a relinquished religion turn into devils."

5. Of course, there are also other motives at the root of this precept forbidding the representation of God, above all the struggle against idolatry (and against the blasphemy of reducing the "infinite" to the dimensions of an image). For Jews, a Catholic procession with its reliquaries and its statues evokes a return to paganism.

References

CHAPTER 1: FREUD AND FEMALE SEXUALITY

Aeschylus. *Eumenides* (transl. R. Lattimore). Chicago: Modern Library, 1942.

Bachofen, J.J. (1861). *Das Mutterecht,* 2 vols. Basle: Benno Schwabe, 1948.

Braunschweig, D. and Fain, M. (1971). *Eros et Anteros.* Paris: Petite Bibl. Payot.

Chasseguet-Smirgel, J. (1964). The feminine guilt and the Oedipus complex. In J. Chasseguet-Smirgel (ed.), *Female Sexuality: New Psychoanalytic Views.* Ann Arbor: Michigan Univ. Press, 1970; London: Karnac Books, 1985.

Freud, S. (1905). Three essays on the theory of sexuality. *S.E.* 7.

Freud, S. (1908). On the sexual theories of children. *S.E.* 9.

Freud, S. (1909). Analysis of a phobia in a five-year-old boy. *S.E.* 10.

Freud, S. (1911). Psycho-analytic notes on an autobiographical account of a case of paranoia (dementia paranoides). *S.E.* 12.

Freud, S. (1915). Instincts and their vicissitudes. *S.E.* 14.

Freud, S. (1917). A metapsychological supplement to the theory of dreams. *S.E.* 14.

Freud, S. (1918). From the history of an infantile neurosis. *S.E.* 17.

Freud, S. (1920). Beyond the pleasure principle. *S.E.* 18.

Freud, S. (1923). The infantile genital organization: an interpolation into the theory of sexuality. *S.E.* 19.

Freud, S. (1924). The dissolution of the Oedipus complex. *S.E.* 19.

Freud, S. (1925). Some psychical consequences of the anatomical distinction between the sexes. *S.E.* 19.

Freud, S. (1926). Inhibitions, symptoms and anxiety. *S.E.* 20.

Freud, S. (1931). Female sexuality. *S.E.* 21.

Freud, S. (1933). New introductory lectures on psychoanalysis: XXXIII. Femininity. *S.E.* 22.

Freud, S. (1937). Analysis terminable and interminable. *S.E.* 23.

Freud, S. (1940). An outline of psycho-analysis. *S.E.* 23.

Freud, S. (1950). Project for a scientific psychology. *S.E.* 1.

Gillespie, W. (1975). Woman and her discontents. A reassessment of Freud's views on female sexuality. *Int. Rev. Psycho-Anal.* 2, 1–9.

Grunberger, B. (1956). La situation analytique et le processus de guérison. In *Le Narcissisme*. Paris: Payot, 1971; New York: I.U.P., 1979.

Grunberger, B. (1966). Oedipe et narcissisme. In *Le Narcissisme*. Paris: Payot, 1971; New York: I.U.P., 1979.

Jones, E. (1933). The phallic phase. *Int. J. Psycho-Anal.* 14, 1–33.

McDougall, J. (1972). Primal scene and sexual perversion. *Int. J. Psycho-Anal.* 53, 371–384.

CHAPTER 2: THE FEMININITY OF THE ANALYST IN PROFESSIONAL PRACTICE

Chasseguet-Smirgel, J. (1964). *Female Sexuality: New Psychoanalytic Views*. London: Karnac Books, 1985.

———(1974). Perversion, idealization and sublimation. *Int. J. Psychoanal.*, 55:349–357.

———(1978). Reflections on the connexions between perversion and sadism. *Int. J. Psychoanal.*, 59:27–35.

David C. (1975). La bisexualité psychique. *Rev. Franç. Psychanal.*, 39:695–856.

Ferenczi, S. (1913). Stages in the development of the sense of reality. In *First Contributions to Psycho-Analysis*. London: Hogarth Press, pp. 213–239.

———(1924). Thalassa. A Theory on Genitality. New York: *The Psychoanalytic Quarterly*, 1938.

Freud, S. (1905). Three essays on the theory of sexuality. *S.E.* 7.

———(1913). The disposition of obsessional neurosis. *S.E.* 12.

———(1915). Instincts and their vicissitudes. *S.E.* 14.

———(1915). The unconscious. *S.E.* 14.

————(1918). From the history of an infantile neurosis (The Wolf-Man). *S.E.* 17.

————(1919). The 'Uncanny'. *S.E.* 17.

————(1920). Beyond the pleasure principle. *S.E.* 18.

————(1923). Two encyclopaedia articles. A Psycho-analysis. *S.E.* 18.

————(1925). Some psychical consequences of the anatomical distinction between the sexes. *S.E.* 19.

————(1933). Femininity. *S.E.* 22.

Greenacre, P. (1954). The role of transference: practical considerations in relation to psycho-analytic therapy. *J. Amer. Psychoanal. Assn.*, 2:671–684.

Grunberger, B. (1956). The analytic situation and the dynamics of the healing process. In *Narcissism: Psychoanalytic Essays.* New York: Int. Univ. Press, 1979, pp. 35–89.

————(1982). Narcisse et Anubis *Revue Française de Psychanalyse,* pp. 921–938.

Horney, K. (1932). The dread of woman. *Int. J. Psychoanal.*, 13:348–360.

Kestenberg, J. (1956). Vicissitudes of female sexuality. In *Children and Parents.* New York: Aronson, 1975, pp. 3–24.

Klein, M. (1945). The Oedipus complex in the light of early anxieties. In *Contributions to Psycho-Analysis.* London: Hogarth Press, 1948, pp. 339–390.

Sharpe, E. (1930). The technique of psycho-analysis. I. The analyst—essential qualifications for the acquisition of technique. In *Collected Papers on Psycho-Analysis.* London: Hogarth Press, 1950, pp. 9–21.

Stoller, R. (1968). *Sex and Gender.* New York: Science House.

Van der Sterren, D. (1974). *Ödipus.* München: Taschenbücher.

CHAPTER 3: SUBMISSIVE DAUGHTERS

Bick, E. (1968) The experience of the skin in early object relations, *Int. J. of Psycho-Anal.,* 49, 484–486

Fernandez, D. (1982) *Dans la main de l'ange,* Paris: Grasset

Freud, S. (1914) On Narcissism: An Introduction, *S.E.,* 14

Freud, S. (1915) Instincts and their Vicissitudes, *S.E.,* 14

Letarte, P. (1973) L'Idéal du Moi et la peur d'être englouti in *Revue Française de Psychanalyse,* 37, 1134–1136

Lewin, K., (1951) *The Psycho-Analysis of Elation,* London: Hogarth Press

McDougall, J. (1964) Homosexuality in women, in J. Chasseguet-Smirgel, *Female Sexuality,* London: Karnac Books, 1985 (3rd edition)

Schreber, D.P. (1903) *Memoirs of my Nervous Illness,* Cambridge Ma: R. Bentley, 1955

CHAPTER 4: ON TRANSFERENCE LOVE IN THE MALE

Baudelaire, C. (1857) *Les Fleurs du Mal,* Paris: Belles Lettres, 1952

Chasseguet-Smirgel, J. (1964) Feminine Guilt and the Oedipus Complex in *Female Sexuality,* London: Karnac Books, 1985

Chasseguet-Smirgel, J. (1985) *Creativity and Perversion,* London: Free Association Books; New York: Norton.

Freud, S. (1915) Observations on Transference Love, *S.E.,* 14

Freud, S. (1916–1917) *Introductory Lectures on Psycho-Analysis, S.E.,* 15

Freud, S. (1917) On Transformations of Instinct as exemplified in Anal Eroticism, *S.E.,* 16.

Freud, S. (1919) The 'Uncanny,' *S.E.,* 17

Freud, S. (1921) Group Psychology and the Analysis of the Ego, *S.E.,* 18

Freud, S. (1925) Some Psychical Consequences of the anatomical distinction between the sexes, *S.E.,* 19

Freud, S. (1933) Femininity in *New Introductory Lectures, S.E.,* 22

Grunberger, B. (1971) *Narcissism,* New York: International Universities Press, 1979

Segal, H. (1953) A psycho-analytic approach to aesthetics in *Intern. J. of Psychoan.,* 33:196–207

CHAPTER 5: THE ARCHAIC MATRIX OF THE OEDIPUS COMPLEX

Chasseguet-Smirgel, J. (1978) Reflections on the Connections between Sadism and Perversion, *International Journal of Psycho-Analysis,* 59:27–35

Chasseguet-Smirgel, J. (1984) Perversion and the Universal Law, *Creativity and Perversion,* New York: Norton.

Ferenczi, S. (1924) Thalassa. A Theory on Genitality, *Psycho-Analytic Quarterly,* 1938

Freud, S. (1909) *The Interpretation of Dreams, S.E.,* 5

Freud, S. (1911) Formulations on the Two Principles of Mental Functioning, *S.E.,* 12

Freud, S. (1917) Introductory Lectures on Psycho-Analysis, *S.E.* 16, p. 397

Freud, S. (1920) Beyond the Pleasure Principle, *S.E.,* 18

Freud, S. (1923) The Ego and the Id, *S.E.,* 19

Freud, S. (1924) Open Letter, February 15, in Jones, E. *Sigmund Freud, Life and Work III,* London: Hogarth Press, 1957

Freud, S. (1924) Neurosis and Psychosis, *S.E.,* 19

Freud, S. (1924) The Economic Problem of Masochism, *S.E.,* 19

Freud, S. (1926) Inhibitions, Symptoms and Anxiety, *S.E.,* 20

Freud, S. (1939) Moses and Monotheism, *S.E.,* 23 p. 120

Grunberger, B. (1983) Narcisse et Anubis, *Revue Française de Psychanalyse,* pp. 921–938

Kernberg, O. (1975) *Borderline Conditions and Pathological Narcissism,* New York: Jason Aronson

Klein, M. (1928) The early stages of the Oedipal conflict, *Contributions to Psycho-Analysis,* London: The Hogarth Press, 1948

Klein, M. (1930) The importance of symbol-formation in the development of the ego, *Contributions to Psycho-Analysis,* London: The Hogarth Press, 1948

Klein, M. (1930) Psychotherapy of psychoses, *Contributions to Psycho-Analysis,* London: The Hogarth Press, 1948

Klein, M. (1932) The first stages of the Oedipus conflict and the formation of the superego, *Psycho-analysis of Children.*

Rank, O. (1924) *The Trauma of Birth.*

Segal, H. (1957) Notes on Symbol formation in *Intern. J. of Psycho. Anal.,* 38:391–397

CHAPTER 6: THE ARCHAIC MATRIX OF THE OEDIPUS COMPLEX IN UTOPIA

Bernardin de Saint Pierre, J.H. (1788) *Paul et Virginie,* Paris: Larousse

Cohn, N. (1957) *The Pursuit of the Millennium,* London: Secker and Warburg

Fourier, C. (1808) *Théorie des quatre mouvements,* Paris: J.J. Pauvert, 1967

More, T. (1515) *Utopia,* London: Dent, 1957

Plato (c. 400 B.C.) *La République* in *Oeuvres complètes,* Paris: Pléiade/Gallimard

Plato (c. 400 B.C.) *Les Lois* in *Oeuvres complètes,* Paris: Pléiade/Gallimard

Rousseau, J.J. (1759) *La nouvelle Héloïse* in *Oeuvres complètes,* Paris: Pléiade/Gallimard, trans. Everyman's Library

Rousseau, J.J. (1760) *Le contrat social* in *Oeuvres complètes,* Paris: Pléiade/Gallimard, trans. Everyman's Library

Rousseau, J.J. (1761) *Emile* in *Oeuvres complètes,* Paris: Pléiade/Gallimard, trans. Everyman's Library

Sade, D.A.F. (1788) *La nouvelle Justine ou les malheurs de la Vertu, VI* in *Oeuvres complètes,* Paris: Cercle du Livre Précieux/Tchou, 1967

Servier, J. (1967) *Histoire de l'Utopie,* Paris: Idées/Gallimard

Yathay, P. (1980) *L'Utopie meurtrière,* Paris: Laffont

Zamiatine, Y. (1924) *We,* London: Penguin Books, 1972

CHAPTER 7: "THE GREEN THEATER"

Appel, R. (1985) "Weh dem, Enkel ist" in *Frankfurter Allgemeine,* August 6, 1985

Brainin, E., Kaminer, I. (1984) "La Psychanalyse et le National Socialism" in *Ecrits du Temps,* No. 6

Chasseguet-Smirgel, J. (1973–85) *The Ego Ideal,* London: Free Association Books; New York: Norton

Fischer, J. (1984) *Von grüner Kraft und Herrlichkeit,* Hamburg: Rowohlt

Freud, S. (1911) "The Schreber Case" in *S.E.* 12

Glücksmann, A. (1984) *La force du vertige,* Paris: Fayard

Grünen (Green Movement), various pamphlets including: Die Grünen: *Das Bundesprogramm;* GAL: *Programm für Hamburg*

Klein, H. (1983) personal correspondence

Lanzmann, C. (1985) *Shoah,* Paris: Fayard

Mann, T. (1948, 1985) *Appels aux Allemands 1940–1945,* Paris: Balland/Martin Flinker

——(1938) "A Brother" in *The Order of the Day,* trans. H.T. Lowe-Porter et al., New York: Alfred Knopf, 1942

Sandoz, G. (1980) *Ces Allemands qui ont défié Hitler,* Paris: Pygmalion

Sauzay, B. (1985) *Le vertige allemand,* Paris: Olivier Orban

Walser, M. (1961) "Schwarzer Schwann" in *Gesammelte Werke,* 1982, Frankfurt am Main: Suhrkamp Verlag

CHAPTER 8: THE PARADOX OF THE FREUDIAN METHOD

Anzieu, D. (1975) *L'auto-analyse de Freud,* 2 vol., Paris: Presses Universitaires de France

Beguin, A. (1937–39) *L'âme romantique et la rêve,* Paris: José Corti

Carus, C.G. (1820) *Letters on Landscape Painting*

Chasseguet-Smirgel, J. (1973) L'idéal du Moi: Essai sur la maladie d'Idéalité, in *Revue Française de Psychanalyse,* 1974

——(1982) *Das Ich-Ideal,* Frankfurt, Suhrkamp Verlag

——(1984) Perversion and the Universal Law in *Creativity and Perversion,* London: Free Association Books; New York: Norton

——(1985) *The Ego-Ideal,* London: Free Association Books; New York: Norton

Deleuze, G. and Guattari, F. (1972) *L'Anti-Oedipe,* Paris: Editions de Minuit

Deutsch, Grand Rabbi, (1977) *Manuel d'instruction religieuse israëlite,* Paris: Fondation Sefer

Fichte, J.G. (1807–1808) *Discours à la Nation Allemande,* Paris: Aubier-Montaigne, 1981

Freud, S. (1911) The two principles of mental functioning, *S.E.* 11

——(1912–1913) Totem et Tabou, *S.E.* 13

——(1922) Article Psycho-Analysis in Encyclopaedia, *S.E.* 18

——(1925) Autobiographical Study, *S.E.* 20

——(1927) The Future of an Illusion, *S.E.* 21

——(1929) Civilization and its Discontent, *S.E.* 21

——(1932–1933) New Introductory Lectures, *S.E.* 22

——(1907–1926) *Correspondence Sigmund Freud–Karl Abraham*

——(1909–1939) *Psychoanalysis and Faith, The Letters of Sigmund Freud and Oskar Pfister,* New York: Basic Books, 1963

——(1927–1939) *Correspondence Sigmund Freud–Arnold Zweig* Paris: Gallimard

Heine, H. *Prose Writings of Heine,* trans. Havelock Ellis in Camelot

Series "The Jewish People", ed. Ernest Rhys, New York: Arno Press, 1973

———*Religion v. Philosophy in Germany,* trans. John Snodgrass, Beacon Press (U.S.) 1959

———*Complete Poems,* trans. Hal Draper, Suhrkamp/Insel. Pub. Boston Inc. 1982

Mann, T. (1926) Les tendances spirituelles de l'Allemagne aujourd'hui in *Thomas Mann Cahiers de l'Herne,* Paris: L'Herne, 1973

———(1929) Freud's Position in the History of Modern Thought in *Past Masters and Other Papers,* trans. H.T. Lowe-Porter, Martin Secker

———(1930) Les arbes de l'Eden in *Les exigences du jour,* Paris: Grasset, 1970

———(1930) An Appeal to Reason in *The Order of the Day,* trans. H.T. Lowe-Porter et al. New York: Alfred Knopf, 1942

———(1931) The Rebirth of Decency in *Les exigences du jour,* Paris: Grasset, 1970

———(1933–1934) Germany My Affliction

———(1935) Europe Beware in *The Order of the Day*

———(1936) Freud et l'avenir in *Nobleness of Spirit,* Paris: Albin Michel, 1960

———(1938) A Brother in *The Order of the Day*

———(1941–1945) *Appels aux Allemands 1940–1945,* Paris: Balland/Flinker, 1985

———(1945) Germany and the Germans in USA Congress Library

———(1949) *The Genesis of a Novel,* trans. R. and C. Winston, New York: Alfred Knopf, 1961

Minder, R. (1936) *Ludwig Tieck,* Paris

Moritz, K.P. (1785–1790) *Anton Reiser*

———(1790) *The Diary of a Visionary*

———(1785 and 1790) *Andreas Hartknopf,* 2 vols.

Papaioannou, K. (1962) *Hegel,* Paris: Seghers

Vermorel, H. and M. (1985) *Freud romantique?*

Wulff, M. (1945) Prohibition against Simultaneous Consumption of Milk and Flesh in Orthodox Jewish Law, in *International Journal of Psycho-Analysis,* 26, pp. 169–176

Zweig, A. Freud's Odyssey in *Die psychoanalytishe Bewegung,* Berlin, 4th year, March–April 1932, no. 2

Index